FIRST *Art* KIT

FIRST *Art* KIT

25 CREATIVE PAPERCRAFT REMEDIES FOR WHAT AILS YOU

Boo Paterson

TILLER PRESS

New York   London   Toronto   Sydney   New Delhi

TILLER PRESS

An Imprint of Simon & Schuster, Inc.
1230 Avenue of the Americas
New York, NY 10020

This publication contains the opinions and ideas of its author. It is intended to provide helpful and informative material on the subjects addressed in the publication. It is sold with the understanding that the author and publisher are not engaged in rendering medical, health, or any other kind of personal professional services in the book. The reader should consult his or her medical, health, or other competent professional before adopting any of the suggestions in this book or drawing inferences from it.

The author and publisher specifically disclaim all responsibility for any liability, loss, or risk, personal or otherwise, which is incurred as a consequence, directly or indirectly, of the use and application of any of the contents of this book.

First Tiller Press hardcover edition May 2021

TILLER PRESS and colophon are trademarks of Simon & Schuster, Inc.

For information about special discounts for bulk purchases, please contact Simon & Schuster Special Sales at 1-866-506-1949 or business@simonandschuster.com.

The Simon & Schuster Speakers Bureau can bring authors to your live event. For more information or to book an event, contact the Simon & Schuster Speakers Bureau at 1-866-248-3049 or visit our website at www.simonspeakers.com.

Interior design by Jennifer Chung

Manufactured in China

1 3 5 7 9 10 8 6 4 2

Library of Congress Cataloging-in-Publication Data
Names: Paterson, Boo, author.
Title: First art kit : creative papercraft remedies for what ails you / Boo Paterson.
Description: New York : Tiller Press, 2021. | Includes bibliographical references.
Identifiers: LCCN 2020034582 (print) | LCCN 2020034583 (ebook) | ISBN 9781982152727 (hardcover) | ISBN 9781982152734 (ebook) Subjects: LCSH: Paper work. | Self-actualization (Psychology).
Classification: LCC TT870 .P385 2021 (print) | LCC TT870 (ebook) | DDC 745.54—dc23

LC record available at https://lccn.loc.gov/2020034582
LC ebook record available at https://lccn.loc.gov/2020034583

ISBN 978-1-9821-5272-7

This book is dedicated to my late,
great friend Michael Seidenberg,
the owner of New York's secret bookshop
and raconteur extraordinaire

CONTENTS

✚ INTRODUCTION

IN LIFE, WE ALL EXPERIENCE moments of joy as well as sadness. Having a range of emotions is normal and part of what makes us human. As an artist, one thing that has always helped me to weather any emotional storms is the creation of art. The process of being creative gives me a sense of accomplishment and mastery, as well as a space to clear my mind and think of nothing else but making. Although I'm not a trained therapist or licensed practitioner, I want to share what I've learned and how I've made my way through.

I came up with the idea of *First Art Kit* because I've endured many difficult times in my life and, to overcome my problems, have engaged in multiple types of therapy, which have by and large been very useful. When I was at one particularly fraught crisis point, I decided to "fix" myself by writing down a list of all the strategies I had learned in therapy and then creating accompanying papercraft artworks that reminded me of what I'd learned in order to help me focus on a way out of my situation. Not only did this help me recover from my predicament but it also helped me realize that many of my own difficulties were universal—and thus this "first aid kit for the soul" was born. That is to say, as you flip through this book, rather than finding bandages and iodine inside, instead you'll find twenty-five creative papercraft remedies and advice for addressing common problems related to mental health.

Each papercraft's chapter in *First Art Kit* is divided into four sections. The opening paragraph describes an issue you may be dealing with as well as its causes and effects. "First Steps" then outlines common psychological techniques, many of which I've used, to help address the issue. "First Art Kit Remedy" comes next, and that consists of therapeutic advice I've received from professionals over the years that has worked for me. This is tied to the last section: the creation of the papercraft. For each craft, I've provided a list of tools you will need and a photo of the finished papercraft for your reference. In many of the chapters, I've also provided true-to-size templates of certain elements that you can trace or photocopy in order to make the papercraft exactly as I did.

The making of the papercrafts in this book is enjoyably beneficial in itself, as it allows you to enter a "flow state," which is a frame of mind where you don't notice time passing because you're so absorbed in the task. In their finished form, the crafts also serve as important reminders for you to challenge any unhelpful thoughts or behaviors that are negatively impacting your life.

Rather than being a total cure or a substitute for therapy, *First Art Kit* should be thought of as a nudge in the right direction. I hope it can be of use to those in need, open up a conversation about mental health, and encourage those who are really struggling with a particular issue to seek further help. There's no shame in having a problem and getting professional treatment for it. Good mental health is something everyone deserves.

HOW TO PAPERCUT

AS SOME OF THE CRAFTS in this book involve the practice of papercutting, here are some helpful papercutting tips as well as guidelines for properly and safely using traditional papercutting tools.

- Before you begin papercutting, always place a cutting mat on a sturdy table that doesn't move when you press down on it. Hold your papercutting implement—such as a craft knife or scalpel—almost as you would a pen. Your index finger can sit on the long support behind the blade but never on the blade itself.

- When papercutting, you should always cut toward yourself, turning the mat so that you are cutting downward each time. Keep your free hand above or to the side of the cut that you're making to steady the paper.

- The general rule in papercutting is to start in the middle and work your way outward. Cut the smallest details first, as the more the cut progresses, the more unstable the paper becomes and the harder it is to cut small things.

- Remember to cut slowly and with an even pressure. When you're using a new blade, you will need very little pressure.

- If the idea of using papercutting implements like craft knives and scalpels makes you feel uncomfortable, there are plenty of other papercrafts for you to do in this book that do not involve or require them.

- For more information on how to safely hold, use, and take care of papercutting implements, head to boopaterson.com for video tutorials.

TOOLS

BELOW IS A HANDY LIST of all the tools and materials I used to make the papercrafts in this book. You can also find papercraft-specific tool lists in each chapter.

- 12" pipe cleaners
- 18" x 12" cutting mat
- Awl
- Battery-operated pillar candle or tea light, 5 cm in diameter or less
- Bulldog clips (small)
- Colored construction paper
- Colored paper
- Colored pencils or pens
- Craft knife
- Embroidery thread
- Eraser
- Felt pen (black)
- Foam squares
- Gold paper
- Mass-market paperback book (damaged)
- Masking tape
- Metallic paper
- Needle and thread
- No. 3 scalpel
- No. 11 blade
- Pencil
- Plain white paper
- Ribbon or long strip of colored paper
- Ruler
- Scissors
- Spray mount adhesive
- Stapler
- Stick or PVA glue
- String
- Thick card, such as mount board, or bamboo skewers
- Thin card, such as paperboard
- Thin metallic card
- Tracing paper
- Watercolor or pastel paper
- Wite-Out

One

PRIORITIZE YOUR NEEDS AND FIND SELF-FULFILLMENT

While it's obviously good to be a kind and giving person, some of us give so much that we neglect our own needs and push ourselves to constantly be productive. Failure to prioritize your needs can lead to feeling resentful or drained of energy and can contribute to anxiety and a persistent feeling of sadness or depression.

The critical voice in your head saying you're not good enough is often the culprit, but self-care is actually essential for being able to have a happy life and give the best of yourself to others.

+ FIRST STEPS

One way to start prioritizing your needs is to do more of what you love— and even schedule it in if you feel you can't make time for it. Make a list of all the pleasurable things you have always wanted to do, as well as all the little things that make you happy but that you cast aside as unimportant in your stress-head, overachievement mode.

It can be as simple as delegating time to read a book in the bath or to sit in the park and watch the world go by. Whatever it is that floats your boat—resolve to do more of it every single day.

If you find it hard to do this or feel guilty taking time for yourself, start with small amounts of time—say, ten minutes a day—then work up to an hour or more.

+ FIRST ART KIT REMEDY

Meeting your own needs isn't selfish—it's instrumental for having good mental health. When we constantly put others first, we feel worn out, but when we do the things that energize us, we have more enthusiasm to give to others.

It's often seen as acceptable to brag about being stressed or overworked, and if you don't, you're a slacker. But this is not the truth. Taking the time to experience joy, wonder, laughter, and being in the moment is important to living a good life.

Once you get over the guilt of taking time for yourself, you'll eventually look forward to every day as opposed to feeling overwhelmed with stress—because finally there's something in it for you.

Remember that although we often look to others to fulfill us or meet our needs, it's through prioritizing our own needs that we will attract the type of people who will truly enrich our lives.

As a papercraft remedy, I want you to make a rosette ribbon that puts you in first place— because it's only in self-fulfillment that you will be the winner.

METHOD

1. Photocopy or trace the **Center** template on page 3 onto a piece of thin card and cut around the outline.

2. Do the same on a piece of colored paper in your favorite color, and make two copies of the **Ribbon** template on page 3 in the same color.

3. Cut lengthways down the colored paper in 2"-wide strips. Hold one against the back of the cardboard **Center** and pleat the strip—thinner at the bottom, thicker at the top—around the outside rim of the **Center**.

4. Staple the strips to the **Center** at intervals to hold them in place, especially when joining a new strip.

5. Once all the strips have been attached, take your two colored ribbons and staple them to the **Center**, allowing the ends to hang over the pleats.

6. Take your colored paper **Center** piece and write "Me 1st" in the middle, before attaching to the cardboard **Center** with glue.

TOOLS

- ○ Thin card, such as paperboard
- ○ Scissors
- ○ Colored paper
- ○ Pencil
- ○ Pen
- ○ Stapler
- ○ Stick or PVA glue

✚

Stick this somewhere prominent in your home as a daily reminder to prioritize your own needs.

CENTER

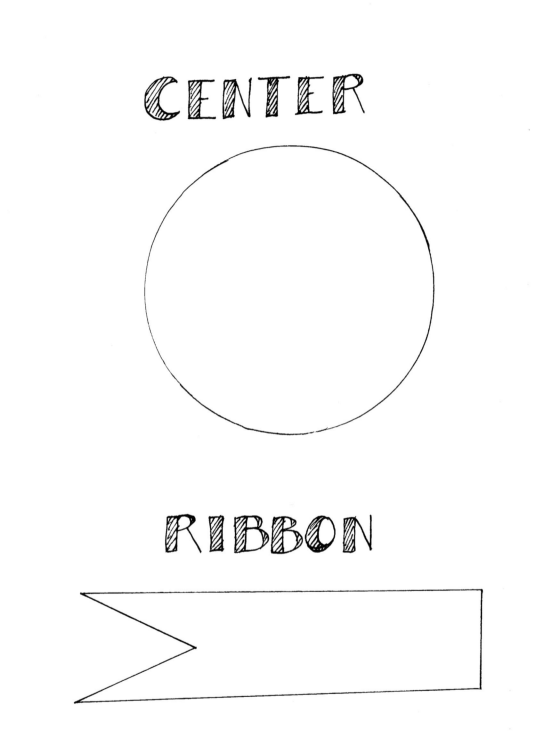

RIBBON

Two

REMEMBER YOUR GREAT QUALITIES WHEN YOU'RE FEELING BLUE

Everyone feels blue occasionally, such as after an upsetting event or major life change, and it's completely normal to feel this way. However, low moods can sometimes seemingly happen for no obvious reason and lead to anxiety, tiredness, anger, or a loss of confidence.

   During these times, it's important to be kind to yourself, do things that improve your mental well-being, and remember what makes you great. If you continue to feel blue despite trying to boost your spirits, I encourage you to talk with a therapist or medical professional.

+ FIRST STEPS

The keys to beating low mood are self-care, routine, and focusing on the positive things you do. Make a list of activities you enjoy and schedule in at least one of these per day. Force yourself to get some exercise, too. Even if you don't feel like moving, you'll feel better afterward.

Feeling low is often caused by unhelpful thoughts, so try to challenge these and reframe your negative perceptions of things. Focus on what you're doing right, not what you're doing wrong, and at the end of each day write down three things you did well—no matter how small they were.

Worrying about the future causes anxiety, and a lack of routine can exacerbate this. Create a plan for each day to give you a feeling of control over the direction of your life.

+ FIRST ART KIT REMEDY

You may feel like you don't have enough time in your day, but taking just ten or fifteen minutes to yourself is better than nothing. Maybe you could read a good novel during your work break, or take a pocket-size sketchbook with you to draw passengers on public transportation.

In a bid to boost your mood, I've illustrated a template of a list of the top ten things you like about yourself, such as "I am a good friend" and "I am kind." The template can be photocopied and colored in, and then filled in with your responses. Alternatively, you could have a go at illustrating one yourself. Each of my therapists has recommended this list-writing exercise when I've suffered from low mood.

You can then store the list in an envelope—for which I've also provided a template—and take it out whenever the blues strike so you can remind yourself of all your great qualities.

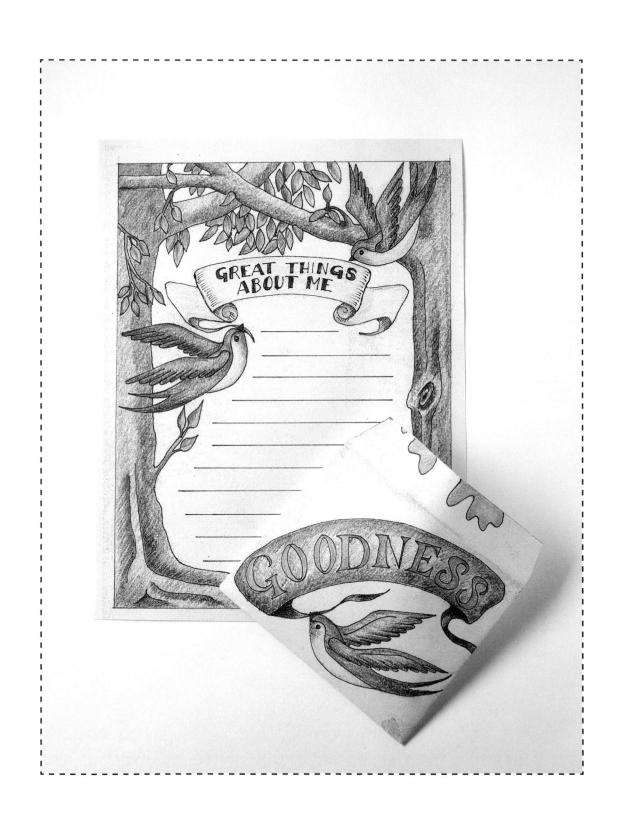

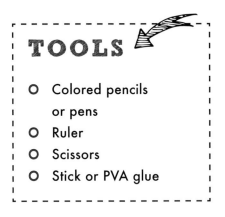

TOOLS

- O Colored pencils
  or pens
- O Ruler
- O Scissors
- O Stick or PVA glue

METHOD

1. Photocopy the templates of the letter and envelope on pages 8 and 9 and color in the line drawings using any colors you like.

2. Put together the envelope by placing a ruler over the dotted lines and using a pair of scissors to score along them.

3. Fold **Tab A** and **Tab B** of the envelope template inward, away from the picture of the swallow. Glue both tabs and fold over the larger panel with oak leaves onto the tabs to create an envelope.

4. Fill in each line of the notepaper with the top ten things you like about yourself today.

5. Store it in the envelope for future reference.

6. Get into the habit of making this list every day so you can appreciate how wonderful you are.

CLEAR YOUR MIND AND GET A GOOD NIGHT'S SLEEP

We've all had those nights when we've tossed and turned for hours, unable to get to sleep. This could be due to bad sleeping habits, noise, or medical conditions keeping you awake—but more commonly it's something that's on your mind.

Being sleepless for one night is bad enough, but habitual sleeplessness, or insomnia, can be long-term, lasting for months or even years. This is why it's important to prioritize getting a good night's sleep.

+ FIRST STEPS

A few natural strategies for dealing with insomnia include making sure your bedroom is a quiet place to relax and sleep and that it's properly dark when you turn out the light. If you have noisy neighbors, try wearing earplugs while you sleep to mitigate the sound.

Wind down and relax at least an hour before bed, and don't use a smartphone, tablet, or TV during that time, as the blue light from these devices can cause you to stay awake.

If you've failed to fall asleep twenty minutes after lights-out, get up and try doing a relaxing activity outside your bedroom, such as reading or crafting, maybe making the 3D sculpture in this chapter.

There are also calming exercises you can do to provoke sleep, such as tensing and relaxing every muscle in your body from the feet up, or imagining yourself walking down a staircase, getting more and more relaxed with every step you take.

+ FIRST ART KIT REMEDY

One therapist-recommended technique I've found very effective is to imagine you're standing in a white room, wearing your favorite clothes, and next to you is a large white box. Into this box you throw every worry that's on your mind—large and small—until you can't think of any more. The worries could involve people, objects, situations, or anxieties—essentially, anything that keeps you awake. Then, you walk over to a cartoon-style TNT detonator at the side of the room and push the plunger down, blowing up the box full of worries.

With this exercise in mind, I want you to make a TNT detonator box (complete with the explosion) to put on your nightstand. This will remind you when you get into bed to get rid of the things causing you anxiety and instead have a restful, worry-free sleep.

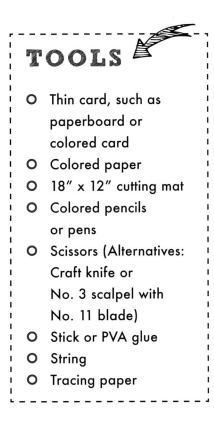

TOOLS

- Thin card, such as paperboard or colored card
- Colored paper
- 18" x 12" cutting mat
- Colored pencils or pens
- Scissors (Alternatives: Craft knife or No. 3 scalpel with No. 11 blade)
- Stick or PVA glue
- String
- Tracing paper

✚

Now you're ready to obliterate your worries and have a peaceful night's sleep!

METHOD

1. Trace the templates on pages 14 and 15 onto colored thin card, or onto paperboard covered with colored paper.

2. Once traced, cut out all the elements. Where the template shows dotted lines, score the rear of the card. Where the template shows a thin black line, cut right through.

3. First, take the **Box** and fold all the dotted lines inward. Glue **Part A** to **Tab A**, **Part B** to **Tab B**, and **Part C** to **Tab C**. The tabs should all end up on the inside of the **Box**.

4. Next, take the **Wingnuts** and insert them into the two smaller slots you cut into the **Box**—**X1** and **X2**. Insert the **Plunger** into the larger slot, marked **X**. Glue the **Strap** to the sides of the **Box** so it curves in between the **Plunger** and the **Wingnuts**.

5. Fold **Tab 1** of the **Flame** backward; this will be used as a stand. Use three-quarters of the **Flame** as a template for the part that's orange in the finished craft photo and flip it over before gluing it to the part that's red in the finished craft photo. Cut out the **Flash** on white and yellow paper, and offset the yellow behind the white as seen in the photo.

6. Finally, glue on the **Bang!** lettering.

7. Take a piece of string and separate it in the middle to create two strands at one end. Tie each strand to a **Wingnut** and glue the other end to the rear of the **Flame**.

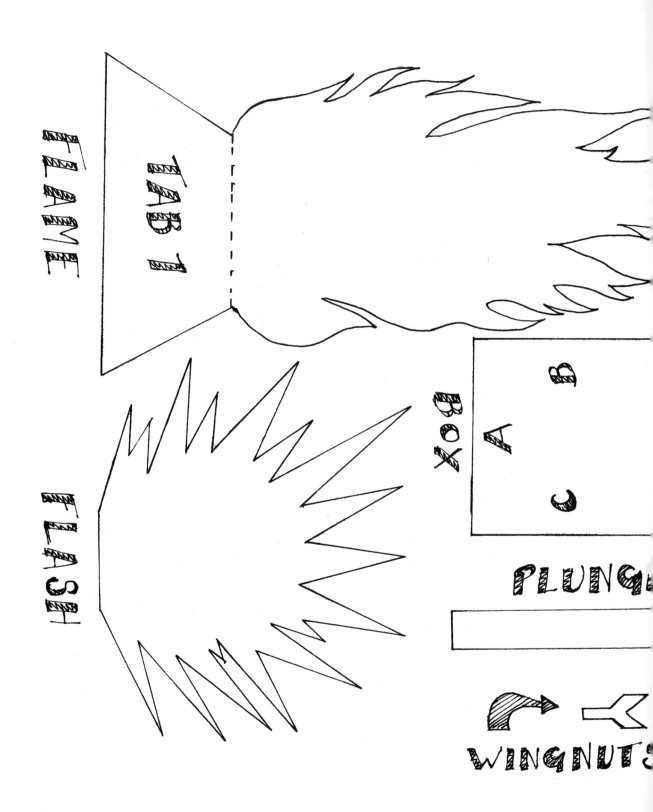

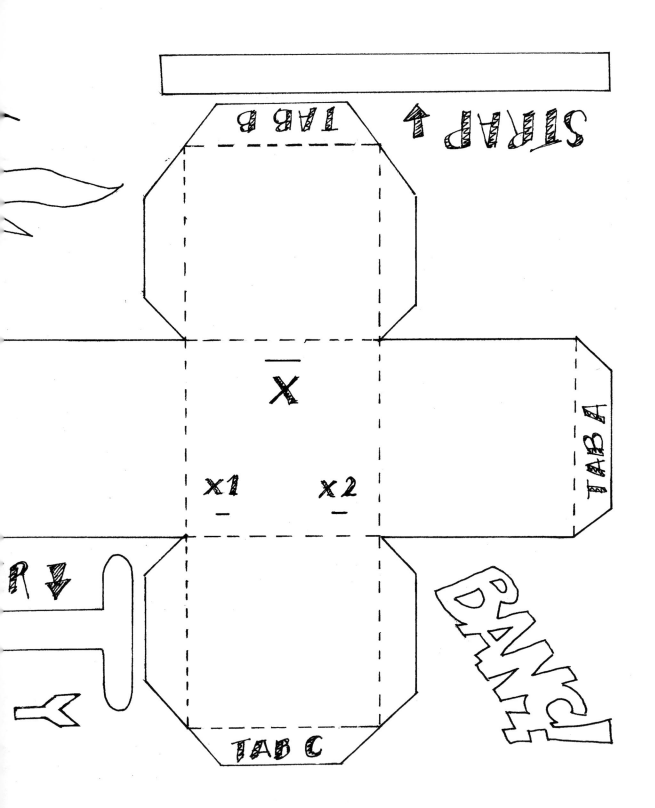

STRAP ↑

TAB B

X

x1   x2

TAB A

BANG!

TAB C

Four

CREATE A RELAXATION TECHNIQUE AND DECREASE ANXIETY

Anxiety is the fear of something going wrong in the future rather than the present, and it can really affect your ability to enjoy life.

Perhaps you feel anxious prior to particular situations, such as going on a date or starting a new job. Or maybe you have an overwhelming sense of doom that affects your whole day and even your sleep. Whatever the cause, there are solutions to this problem, and you are entitled to enjoy your life without the burden of anxiety.

+ FIRST STEPS

Daily exercise is an important strategy in decreasing anxiety, as concentrating on physical movement can give you some respite from being solely in your head.

It can also help to write down what triggers your anxiety so that you can begin to notice patterns and take steps to tackle them before they get out of hand. At the same time, you should also note the good things in your life, too, and make efforts to increase the amount of time you spend on activities that bring you joy.

Relaxation goes hand in hand with this, and many find that practicing yoga, mindfulness, or meditation alleviates their anxiety and helps them cope.

+ FIRST ART KIT REMEDY

Having an effective relaxation technique is essential to dealing with anxiety. One technique that's worked for me is to close your eyes and imagine you are at the top of a sweeping staircase. Beneath your bare feet is a carpet made of red velvet, and the handrail you are holding on to is made of gold.

As you slowly walk down each of the ten steps, feel yourself becoming more and more relaxed. Notice how nice the velvet feels on the soles of your feet and what the gold handrail feels like under your fingers.

At the bottom of the stairs is a pair of grand carved wooden doors with golden handles. You open these doors and walk right out onto a deserted beach, feeling the warmth of the sun on your skin, breathing in the smell of salt water, and hearing the sound of waves lapping gently at the shore. You can stay on this beach, noticing the pleasant aspects, for as long as you like.

This is a great technique to use as you lie down at night if your worries are preventing you from falling asleep. But you can also take ten or twenty minutes during the day to close your eyes and visualize this scene to calm you down.

I've created a tropical beach scene for you to cut into a bas-relief to help you focus on the relaxing rhythm of the sea, the soft sand, and the breeze rustling the leaves of the palm trees.

METHOD

1. Trace or photocopy the template on page 19.

2. Tape construction, watercolor, or pastel paper that is larger than your tracing onto a cutting mat along the paper's edges. Smooth it down with your hands to make sure there are no air bubbles inside.

3. Lay the **Beach** template over the paper, taping its outer edges down in the same way.

4. Holding the scalpel like a pen, begin cutting around all the black elements from the middle of the picture outward.

5. Once you have cut around all the black pieces, carefully peel off the masking tape holding the template down and remove.

6. Then use the tip of the scalpel to pick out the blanks on the colored paper, cutting a little more where pieces may still be joined to the main body of the artwork.

7. Once all the blanks have been removed, take the masking tape and surplus paper off the mat.

8. Pick up the **Beach** scene and gently fold or pinch the paper to give a 3D effect to the elements you want to stand out, such as the waves and the trees.

9. Attach it to a contrasting piece of paper with spray mount adhesive or foam squares.

10. Place your artwork in an area where you experience the greatest amount of anxiety—perhaps by your desk at work—to remind you to go to the beach in your mind whenever you need to.

TOOLS

- O Masking tape
- O Colored construction, watercolor, or pastel paper
- O 18" x 12" cutting mat
- O No. 3 scalpel with No. 11 blade
- O Spray mount adhesive or foam squares

Five

SHOW OFF YOUR SKILLS AND BOOST YOUR SELF-ESTEEM

Many people suffer from low self-esteem, not realizing they're important and talented, and several therapists have told me that one of the most common causes of this is having parents who criticized you too often when you were a child. Additionally, children can be adversely affected by bullying, intense peer pressure, and the tyranny of negative comparisons via social media.

This kind of upbringing can make people really anxious about failure and making mistakes. Those with low self-esteem tend to have little confidence, be very self-critical, and view events and the opinions of others as negative. But those with normal self-esteem have both growth and improvement as their goals, and avoiding failure isn't what drives them.

+ FIRST STEPS

To boost your self-esteem, start by identifying the negative beliefs you have about yourself. Write them down, and then challenge them with the truth.

For example, if you've internalized the thought that you're "stupid," write down all the instances of when you exhibited intelligence or insight, as well as all the nice things people have said about your knowledge or ideas.

Talk to yourself the way you would talk to a good friend you care dearly about—with kindness and compassion—and try to distance yourself from people who bring you down.

Remember that you are as entitled as anyone to have your needs and opinions respected. Assertiveness and confidence are skills you must practice, and the best way to do that is to notice when other people calmly say no or ask for their needs to be met, and then copy what they do.

+ FIRST ART KIT REMEDY

Everyone is good at something, whether it's making people laugh or completing crossword puzzles.

As a remedy, I want you to first spend time thinking about all the things you're good at and all the activities you enjoy. Then, I want you to make yourself the star of your own show—where you are center stage doing something you love—by making this pop-up theater, which you can customize in a way that expresses your boundless creativity.

Paper toy theaters like this were actually popular in Victorian times, when families would put on shows for one another. This one is just for you, though, to remind you how important you are and how many skills you have.

METHOD

1. Trace the templates on pages 24–29 onto colored thin card or paperboard covered with colored paper. Lightly mark the letters and numbers onto the templates in pencil.

2. Cut out all the elements. Where the template shows dotted lines, score the rear of the card. Where the template shows a continuous thin black line, cut right through it. Thick black lines are guidelines for placement of the tabs.

3. Decorate the **Curtain**, **Arch**, and **Backdrop**, or use the **Sunburst** template for the backdrop. I cut mine from colored paper, but you could color in the paper you choose, or fill it in with your own design. You could draw the things you're good at onto the backdrop, or stick on representations of them with cut-out pictures or words from magazines.

4. Don't forget to color in one of the figures. You could do this by sticking colored paper onto the figure to represent your favorite clothes, or you could print out a photo of yourself and stick it on instead. You could even make multiples of the figures for all your friends. Fold the **Tab No. 6** backward and stand them up.

5. Once you've decorated all the elements, you're ready to assemble the theater.

6. Bend **Tab C** on the curtain backward and insert into **Slot C** of the stage. Glue **Tab C** in the backward position.

7. Glue the **Tabs 2** onto the stage and position them behind the **Arch** at the bottom where **2** is marked on the template. Hold in place until set.

TOOLS

- Thin card, such as paperboard or colored card
- Colored paper
- Colored pencils or pens
- 18" x 12" cutting mat
- Scissors (alternatives: craft knife or No. 3 scalpel with No. 11 blade)
- Stick or PVA glue
- Tracing paper

8. Glue **Tabs 1** onto the **Stage** and stick them to the **Back Panel** spaces marked with a **1**.

9. Hold in place until stuck and then wait 30 minutes so the glue can harden before you continue with the craft.

10. Bend **Arch Tab 3**, glue it onto the **No. 3** place on the **Back Panel**, and then rub down this tab under the **Stage** with pencil. Leave glue to harden for 30 minutes.

11. Glue the top **Curtain Tabs B** and **Arch Tab 4** and push **Tab 4** onto the **No. 4** area of the **Back Panel**. At the same time, push the **Curtain Tabs B** up onto the roof of the **Arch** and hold in place until glue sets, then leave for 30 minutes.

12. Glue the rear of the **Backdrop** and slide in behind the **Curtain** onto **No. 5** area of the back panel. This should cover **Tab 4**.

13. Leave glue to dry overnight before folding forward the whole theater to pop up—and put your figure on the stage to remind yourself that you are an amazing person!

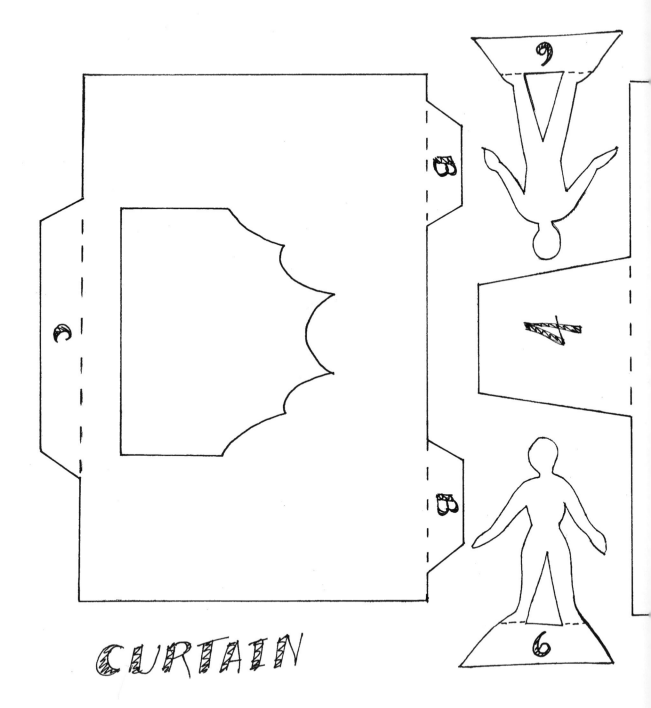

CURTAIN

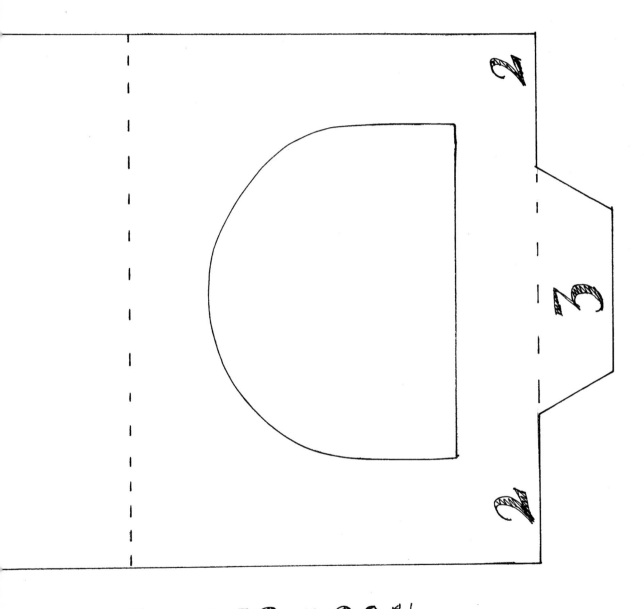

THEATER ARCH

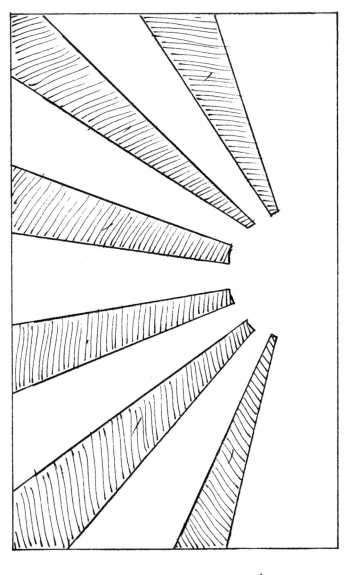

SUNBURST

STA

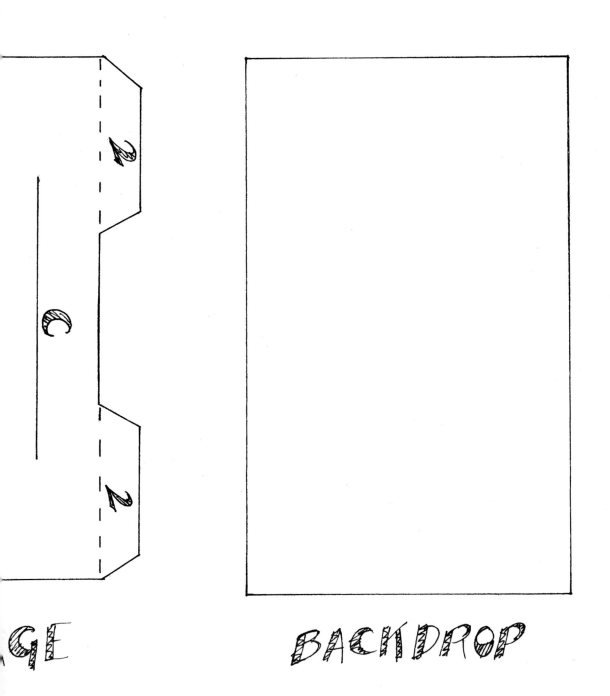

GE

BACKDROP

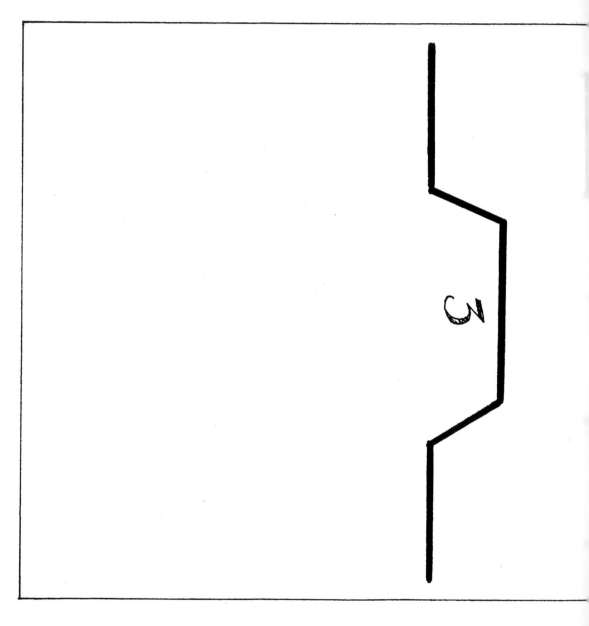

3

BACK

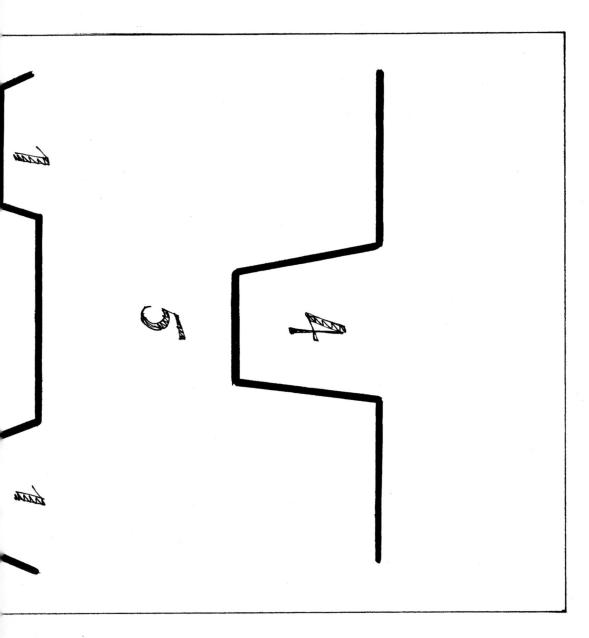

PANEL

Six

RECOVER FROM REJECTION AND RISE LIKE THE PHOENIX

Most of us have experienced the pain of rejection. In fact, research has found that the physical pain pathways in the brain are activated when we feel this emotion, so rejection actively *hurts*.[1]

Suffering a rejection temporarily lowers our IQ, making it difficult to reason, self-soothe, or lower the anger we feel as a common side effect of being rejected.[2] We are also more prone to blame ourselves for rejection, which can damage our self-esteem and prolong recovery times. But when you experience rejection, it's important to remember: you are resilient.

+ FIRST STEPS

Because rejection can be really destabilizing, try, in its wake, to arrange activities with those who love and accept you.

Build your self-esteem back up by writing down your achievements and the things you like about yourself every day. (See chapter 5 for more guidance on boosting self-esteem.)

Try to notice when you talk negatively about yourself, such as when you might say, "It's all my fault," and change that narrative to the more realistic "Everyone experiences rejection—this is part of life."

It can also be useful to give yourself a time frame for your recovery. While you are human and can act emotionally during times of stress, you ultimately are in control of how you behave. So set a literal date and time for letting go of your focus on the rejection. After that date has passed, allow yourself to recognize sad feelings but don't dwell on them.

+ FIRST ART KIT REMEDY

Rejection often takes over our thoughts completely, becoming a kind of obsession, so in order to give you some relief from those thoughts and help you focus deeply on something positive, I have created a phoenix papercut for you to craft.

The phoenix is a mythical bird that was said to live for centuries before it would burst into flames and then rise again from the ashes to experience another cycle of life. My hope is that making this papercraft will allow you to enter an enjoyable "flow" state and give you a sense of achievement upon completion.

We all have much more to give than we realize. Like the phoenix, you will survive rejection and move forward into a more stable future.

TOOLS

- ○ Watercolor or pastel paper
- ○ 18" x 12" cutting mat
- ○ Craft knife or No. 3 scalpel with No. 11 blade
- ○ Masking tape

✚

Place this in an area where you spend most of your day to remind yourself that you'll get stronger and overcome whatever rejection you're going through.

METHOD

1. Tape your colored paper to the cutting mat along the paper's edges. Make sure there are no air bubbles underneath the paper by smoothing it down with your hands.

2. Photocopy the **Phoenix** template on pages 34–35 and lay it over the colored paper, taping its outer edges down in the same way.

3. Starting in the middle of the **Phoenix**, cut all the black lines with either a craft knife or scalpel, holding it like a pen. Leave the outline of the **Phoenix** till last, or else the papercut will become unstable and hard to work on.

4. Once you have cut around all the black pieces, carefully peel off the masking tape that's holding the template down.

5. Then use the tip of the craft knife or scalpel to pick out the blanks on the colored paper, cutting a little more where pieces may still be joined to the main body of the artwork.

6. Once all the blanks have been removed, take the masking tape and surplus paper from the mat.

7. Using the craft knife or scalpel tip, lift up some of the smaller feathers and flames for a bas-relief effect.

8. Then, using your fingers, gently pinch the paper to give definition and a 3D effect to the wings and larger feathers.

9. Finally, bend the paper backward along the dotted lines to allow your **Phoenix** artwork to stand up.

Seven

SURROUND YOURSELF WITH SUPPORTIVE PEOPLE AND STOP SIBLING RIVALRY

Experiencing competition and jealousy with others—especially with brothers and sisters—is very common in childhood. But these feelings can often spill into adulthood as well—even into the workplace, where the hierarchy and office politics are similar to family dynamics.

Sibling rivalry usually starts when one child believes his or her parents favor the child's sibling (or siblings). If this child feels ignored or liked less than his or her sibling(s), then rivalry for the parents' attention often becomes more pronounced. Fighting between kids might also reflect problems in the parents' relationship, as children can end up copying their parents' conflict when acting out.

If you have a similar familial situation, I want you to know that these issues do not have to have power over you.

+ FIRST STEPS

A hierarchy—not favoritism—is important to establish with children in order to show them there are privileges that come with maturing and learning. However, when parents are prone to favoritism, siblings will fight with one another to be seen as unique.

The parent showing favoritism to one child over another may not be aware they are doing so—they may just have more in common with that child or a similar personality. This can lead to conflict and cause not only children but also adults who struggle with a history of past or even current sibling rivalry to feel great anxiety and stress.

If you have such a history, one tactic you can consider using to overcome this struggle is to simply stop competing with your sibling, in the present day or in your memory, and no longer blame them for being "the favorite." By changing your own behavior, you can potentially reset the whole family dynamic, causing other family members to act differently as well.

If this fails, then try to accept the situation as it is and appreciate the elements of your relationship with your parents and your siblings that you do enjoy.

+ FIRST ART KIT REMEDY

Not everyone has a family that supports and encourages them, and if your relationship with your family or siblings only breeds negativity, then it may be best to remove yourself from some or all family members and instead give your attention to those who nurture you.

Appreciate all the good things you have going on in your life and acknowledge you're on your own path, separate from the relatives who may cause you anxiety or hurt. Spend your time and efforts on the people who love and accept you for who you are, whether you're related to them by blood or not.

With this in mind, I want you to make this paper chain of humans to color or collage onto as a representation of all your favorite, supportive people. When you're finished, hang it in a prominent place, such as over a doorway or above the mantelpiece, to remind you that your family is whoever you want it to be!

METHOD

1. Photocopy or trace the template on page 41, then cut out the **Body**.

2. Repeatedly fold a long strip of paper into an accordion that is the same height and width as the template **Body**. The more folds you make, the more figures you'll have.

3. The dotted lines of the **Body**'s hands and feet should line up next to the folded edges of your concertina paper.

4. With a pencil, draw around the **Body** onto the accordion paper, and then cut out around the drawing through all the layers with your scissors.

5. Pull out the chain of people and customize the clothes, hair, and faces with colored pencils or pens or collage colored paper onto it to resemble the people you love the most. You could even cut out photos of these people's faces and stick them over the heads of the people in the chain.

6. I've included some clothes and hair-type templates to get you started. Draw around them onto colored paper, cut them out, and then glue them directly onto the people on your chain.

7. If you need more figures, just add on another paper strip with glue.

8. Once you're finished, thread a needle and poke through the shoulder of the figure on each end. Make a big knot at the end of your thread and pull the rest of it through the figures, which will allow them to be hung as decoration.

TOOLS

- ○ Colored paper
- ○ Pencil
- ○ Scissors
- ○ Colored pencils or pens
- ○ Stick or PVA glue
- ○ Needle and thread

This papercraft is a lovely way to focus on your most positive relationships.

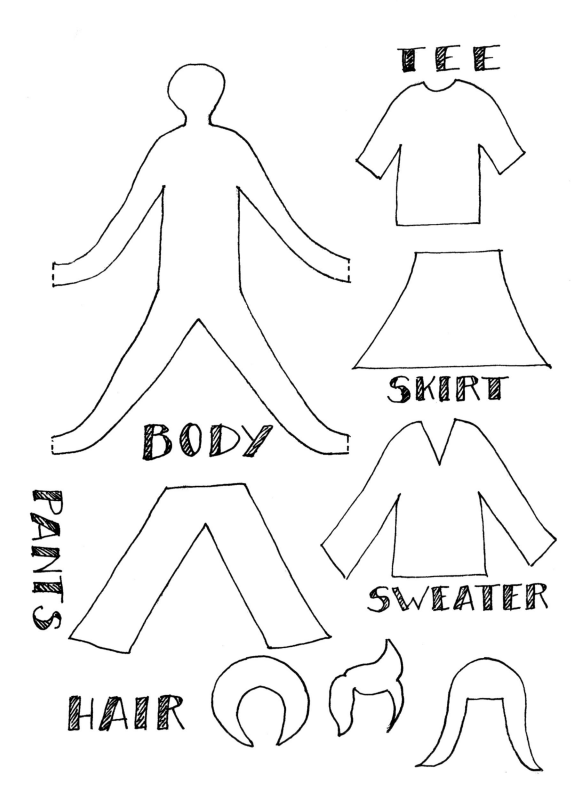

TEE

BODY

SKIRT

PANTS

SWEATER

HAIR

Eight

FREE YOURSELF FROM UNNECESSARY GUILT

Guilt is a tricky emotion that is both good and bad. On one hand, it can motivate you to treat others with respect and to pull your weight, but on the other, it can become a damaging habit that spoils your enjoyment of life.

People often exaggerate guilt-causing offenses in their minds and think they deserve to feel bad for a long time—months or even years—but this is usually far too severe a response to the original misconduct.

If, in your childhood, your parents didn't meet some or all of your basic needs, you may feel guilt over prioritizing yourself. But now that you're an adult, you deserve to nurture those needs, show yourself compassion, and free yourself from unnecessary guilt.

+ FIRST STEPS

No one is perfect all the time—all human beings fail and act in unflattering ways at one point or another—and feeling remorse instead of guilt is a useful way to move forward, as it focuses solely on what you did rather than on your being a bad person in general.

When you feel guilty, accept that the incident happened, apologize to the person you mistreated—even if it's yourself—and work out how to avoid doing it again.

Lastly, if you feel guilty about your behavior toward someone else, be sure to apologize for what the *other person* thinks you did wrong rather than solely what *you* think you did wrong.

+ FIRST ART KIT REMEDY

Question whether the length of time you've felt guilty is appropriate for your wrongdoing. If you notice you feel guilty over the smallest things, it can be useful to write down all the things that you do to help people each day as evidence of your good qualities.

If your guilt is centered around not achieving what you feel you should, maybe consider that the standards that were set by your family when you were a child were just too high. Perhaps these family ideals are not even within your abilities to achieve—and there's nothing wrong with that. We don't all have the same skills, and it would be a very boring world if we did.

Guilt may even rear its ugly head because you're doing things you enjoy. If this is the case, acknowledge the feeling but do the pleasurable activity anyway.

Make this a daily practice, and slowly the feelings of guilt will be overtaken by joy at doing the things you love.

In Buddhism, the fish is a symbol of freedom, happiness, and well-being, so I've created a couple you can make to remind you of these things and that you don't have to constantly be wracked with guilt.

METHOD

1. Trace or photocopy the template on pages 46–47.

2. Tape metallic card that is larger than your tracing onto a cutting mat along its edges. Tape your template over the card along every edge.

3. Holding a craft knife or scalpel like a pen, cut out all the pieces, and score the back of the dotted lines with the back of the blade. Cut all the continuous black lines within the pieces, such as the scales and fins.

4. Once you have cut around all the black lines, carefully peel off the masking tape holding the template down.

5. Take the **Body** of the fish and fold **Tab 1** and **Tab 2** inward. Bend each scale around your index finger from underneath, with your thumb and forefinger pinching over the top, so each scale has a slight bend in it.

6. Glue **Tab 1** and fix it under **Tab 2** to form a cone that's open at both ends. Hold in place until dry or use the bulldog clips to hold the ends in place.

7. Take the **Tail** and bend all the score marks inward. Then push both sides of the **Waist** inward while bending it at the **Hinge**. Glue the **A Tabs** to the **B Tabs** to create a whole tail, and bulldog clip it in place until dry.

8. Take the **Face** and fold inward along all the dotted lines. Fold **Tab 1** and **Tabs A** and **B** inward. Fold the **Fins** outward. Glue together to close the top of the head.

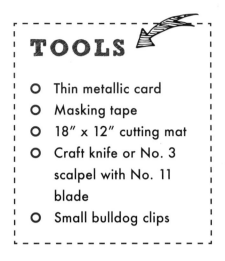

TOOLS

○ Thin metallic card
○ Masking tape
○ 18" x 12" cutting mat
○ Craft knife or No. 3 scalpel with No. 11 blade
○ Small bulldog clips

✚

Display both fish in a prominent place so that whenever those guilty feelings arise, you can choose to be happy instead.

9. Glue **Tab 1** and hold on to its opposite side to create the jaw.

10. Take the **Tail** and bend the fins around your fingers to give shape—I've bent mine so it will stand up on a shelf. Glue the **Tail** at the widest part of the **Hinge** on both sides and slot it into the rear of the **Body**.

11. Fold the **Eyes** inward along the dotted lines. Stick the smaller circles in the center, and then stick each whole **Eye** onto the **Face**.

12. Glue the **Face** along shaded **Part C** and insert into the **Body**, being careful to leave the fins sticking out.

13. To create the smaller fish, photocopy the template at 70 percent and repeat the steps above.

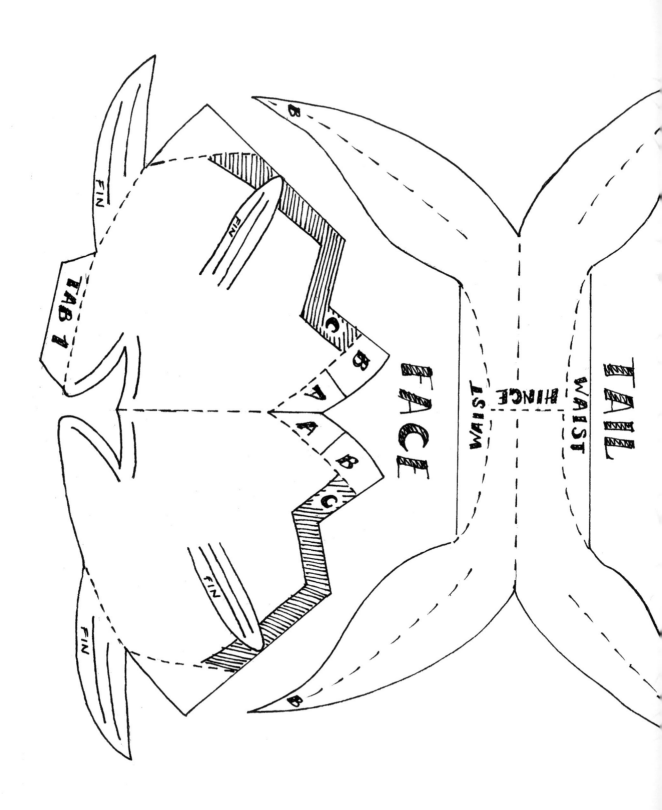

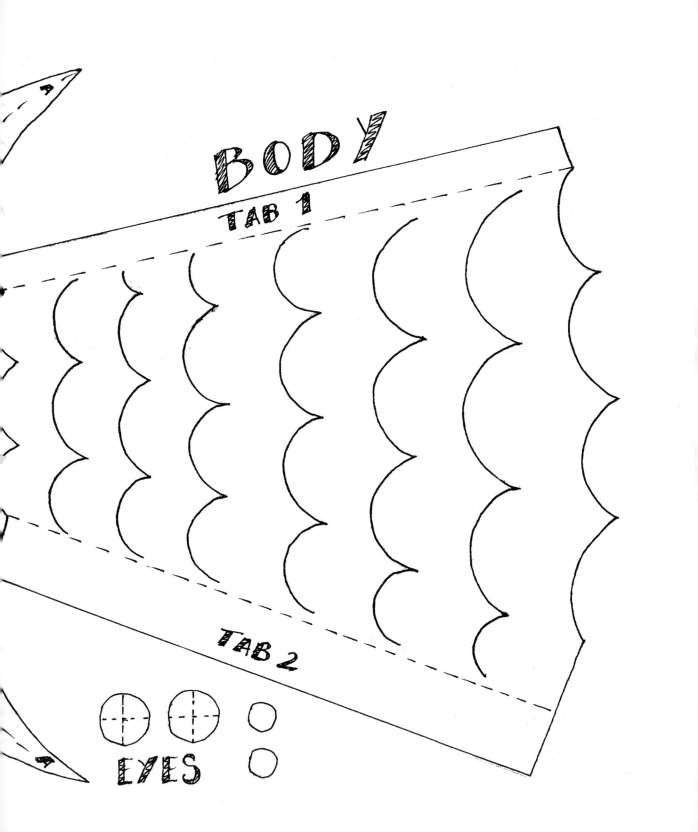

BODY

TAB 1

TAB 2

EYES

FORGIVE YOURSELF AND RELEASE SHAME

Feelings of shame can result in trying to be perfect, holding on to a lot of anger, and being unable to accept any love, positivity, or praise from others—or ourselves. But you have nothing to be ashamed of.

Most shame originates in childhood, when caregivers scold us not for doing something wrong but for being something wrong. Shaming is toxic and can take many forms, but it often manifests in expressions of disgust or the belittling of efforts, ideas, or achievements.

+ FIRST STEPS

Research shows that the more we think or do something, the more those thoughts or actions become habits.[1] So, to begin, change the habit of thinking you're defective. Become more compassionate toward yourself and accept that you are a normal human being with flaws.

Try to challenge that critical voice in your head and think about how you would have liked your caregivers to talk to you as a child. Use that soothing language as your inner voice instead.

The last thing most people want to do is talk about shame—if they even acknowledge it. But discussing it with kind people you trust can help you put it in perspective and show you that you're loved just as you are.

+ FIRST ART KIT REMEDY

If you've been carrying shame around your entire life, it can be hard to challenge the dysfunctional thinking patterns that lead to self-sabotage and imposter syndrome. You may have internalized messages from society about how you should look or act, but you can set yourself free from these expectations by rejecting them and accepting yourself as you are. To be able to move on, you need to first acknowledge this feeling of shame, discuss it with someone sympathetic, and then move on by forgiving yourself and those who made you feel ashamed.

To symbolize forgiveness and talking to someone in confidence without judgment, I've created this 3D, old-timey confessional booth. Once it's completed, you can practice telling the booth your experience of shame before moving on to telling a person you trust.

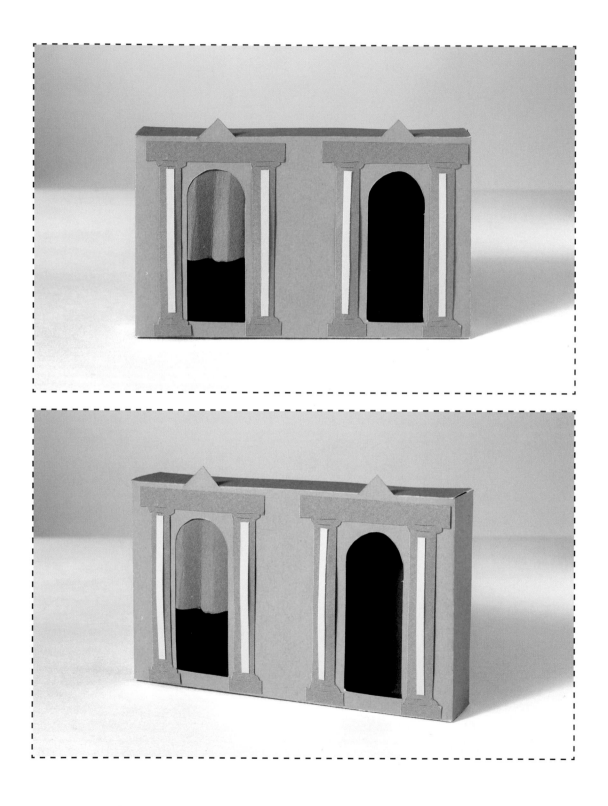

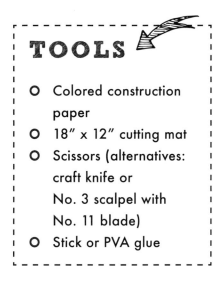

TOOLS

- Colored construction paper
- 18" x 12" cutting mat
- Scissors (alternatives: craft knife or No. 3 scalpel with No. 11 blade)
- Stick or PVA glue

✚

Now you're ready to start letting go of shame – the booth isn't going to tell anyone!

METHOD

1. Photocopy or trace the templates on pages 52–53 onto colored paper. I've used paper that's a different color on each side for the **Booth**, but if you can't get this, you can stick two pieces of different colored paper together before you start.

2. Once the template is traced, mark the letters and numbers on your colored paper, and cut out all the elements, starting with the blacked-out arches of the **Booth**. Where the template shows dotted lines, score the paper. Where the template shows a thin black line, cut right through it.

3. Cut the **Curtain** out of contrasting paper and bend it where you think the folds of the material would go.

4. Fold the **Booth** inward along all the dotted lines, then open it out again and glue the top of the **Curtain** behind one of the arches.

5. Glue the pillars around the arches. I've added a couple of contrasting strips of paper to mine to give them more interest.

6. Glue **Tabs A** and **B** under **Tabs AA** and **BB**, and then glue **Tab 2** under **Tab 1**.

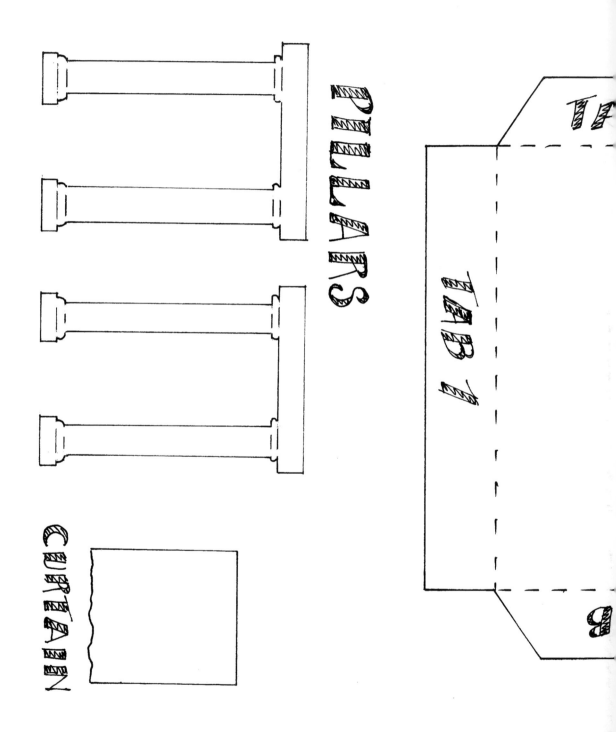

PILLARS

CURTAIN

TAB

TA...

B

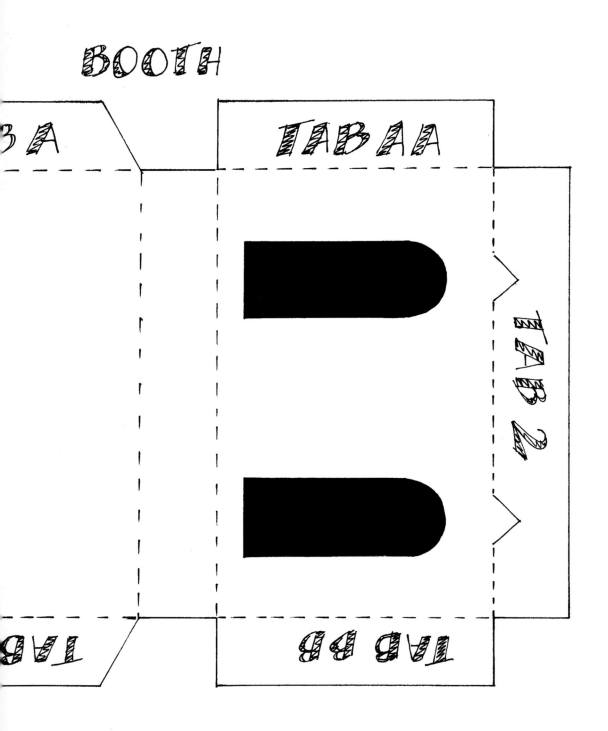

BOOTH

BA

TABAA

TAB 2

TAB BB

TAB

Ten

BRIGHTEN UP YOUR SPACE AND SHAKE OFF SAD

In the depths of winter, when there are shorter days, cold weather, and limited sunlight, many people feel like they have the blues. The symptoms of SAD, or seasonal affective disorder, include feeling down for long periods of time, irritability, a loss of energy, feeling sleepy all the time, craving carbohydrates, and gaining weight.

As well as having a genetic component, it is thought that SAD is linked to reduced exposure to sunlight during the shorter days, and this lack of light may cause part of the brain to malfunction, affecting the body's internal clock and hormones.[1]

Fortunately, there are many practical ways to help shake off SAD.

+ FIRST STEPS

The easiest step to take when dealing with SAD is to go outside and get as much natural sunlight as possible every day. Even on dull days, natural light levels are up to ten times brighter than light that's inside a building—including when you're sitting next to a window. If you can't go outside, I suggest getting a daylight-spectrum lamp especially for SAD sufferers and use this daily until adequate light levels return in spring.

Self-care is also important to keep your mood buoyant. Try doing some physical exercise every day, plan fun activities all through winter to keep your mood up, and take advantage of the available sunlight at every opportunity.

+ FIRST ART KIT REMEDY

The long, cold days of winter can be a real drag, but you're not entirely at the mercy of the darkness.

I've created a papercut 3D lantern shade in the shape of a castle for you to use to brighten up your cozy home and remind you that light comes from within strong defenses.

You can place this papercut around a battery-operated pillar candle or tea light or, alternatively, create some dramatic shadows by placing it near a wall and shining a lamp at it. A lamp shining behind it will give it a different kind of glow.

However you use it, remember the words of the great singer Nina Simone: "Now the summer is gone, there's another to come."

TOOLS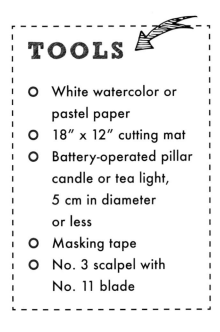

○ White watercolor or pastel paper
○ 18" x 12" cutting mat
○ Battery-operated pillar candle or tea light, 5 cm in diameter or less
○ Masking tape
○ No. 3 scalpel with No. 11 blade

METHOD

1. Trace or photocopy the template on pages 58–59.

2. Along its edges, tape white watercolor or pastel paper that is larger than your tracing onto a cutting mat. Make sure there are no air bubbles inside by smoothing it down with your hands.

3. Lay the **Castle** template over the white paper, taping its outer edges down in the same way.

4. Holding the scalpel like a pen, begin cutting around all the black elements from the middle of the picture outward, leaving the outline of the **Castle** for last.

5. Once you have cut around all the black pieces, carefully peel off the masking tape holding the template down and remove it.

6. Then use the tip of the scalpel to pick out the blanks, cutting a little more where pieces may still be joined to the main body of the artwork.

7. Once all the blanks have been removed, take the remaining masking tape and the surplus paper from the mat.

8. Insert the tab into the slot at the back of the **Castle**, which allows it to form a cylindrical shape and stand up.

9. Turn the flameless light on and place the **Castle** "sleeve" over the top. Keep in mind that the dark days will pass and you'll feel the sun on your face in no time.

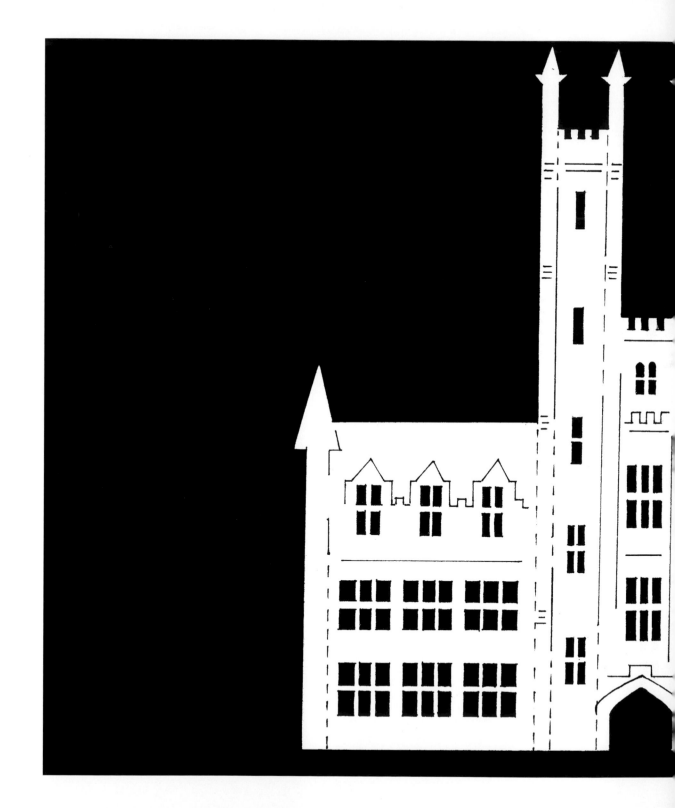

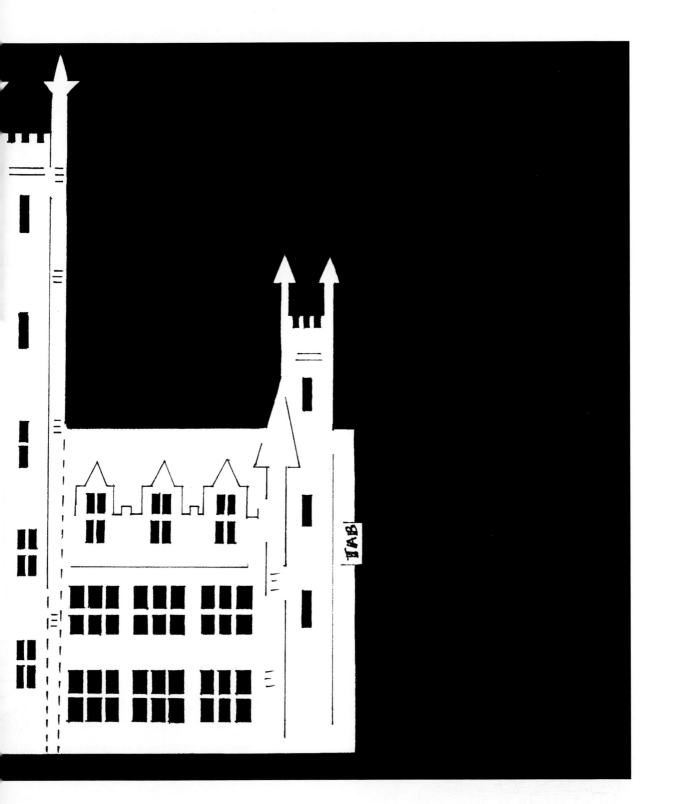

Eleven

REMIND YOURSELF YOU ARE A CHAMPION AND BUILD UP YOUR CONFIDENCE

Everyone has varying levels of confidence in any given task. You can have high self-esteem in general but low confidence in certain situations where you feel unsure or out of your depth.

Many of us—particularly women and certain ethnic groups—are also socialized to believe that we can't do certain things, and that if we try, we will fail. This fear keeps us from even attempting to reach our potential.

The mass media doesn't help either. Advertisers know that if you make people feel like they're lacking in some way, you can sell them a product that fixes that lack. But I'm here to remind you: don't believe the hype!

+ FIRST STEPS

Accomplishments boost confidence, so if you feel you lack self-assurance in a certain arena, begin by setting relatively easy goals for yourself in that area so that you can master each one in turn. Taking these small steps while also monitoring your progress will give you a sense of pride and raise your confidence to keep taking on bigger challenges.

If you feel nervous before embarking on a new goal, try also changing your body language to a "power pose." The most common power pose is to stand with feet shoulder-width apart, chest out, and hands on hips. Staying in this position for a minute or two has been proven to increase the hormones that provide confidence.[1]

+ FIRST ART KIT REMEDY

Start by questioning your beliefs about your abilities and resolving to stick to hard facts that you have tested in the real world.

Having support is not to be underestimated. Talk to your close friends about your lack of confidence and ask them to encourage and correct you when you make statements like "I can't do that."

Stop labeling yourself as someone who "can't" and relabel yourself as someone who "can." Negative self-talk is pointless, and it guarantees you'll never move forward and increase in confidence.

Think of the athletes who are coached to envisage themselves winning. They wouldn't get very far if they kept their expectations in check.

You need to be your own coach, shouting from the sidelines that you can do it, and visualize yourself as someone who's confident and capable. As a way of helping you do this, I want you to create a gold medal to remind yourself that you are entirely capable of becoming a champion, too.

METHOD

1. Trace the templates on page 63 onto gold paper.

2. Cut out **Circle 1** along the continuous outer-edge lines, and then write "Winner" in the center of the circle.

3. Fold the dotted lines of the innermost circle toward the center of the back of the **Medal**—on the opposite side to the "Winner" writing. Then fold the dotted lines of the outer part of the circle inward.

4. Once all the tabs are folded, adjust these so that they make two 45-degree angles, comprising the edge of the **Medal** and a back area to attach **Circle 2** onto.

5. Cut out **Circle 2**, generously glue around the rim, and attach to the tabs at the back of **Circle 1**.

6. As the glue is setting, carefully adjust the rim of the medal and the outer edges of the tabs under **Circle 2** so that all the tabs are covered by it.

7. Thread ribbon or a long piece of paper ¾" wide through the loop at the top of **Circle 2** and hang the medal around your neck.

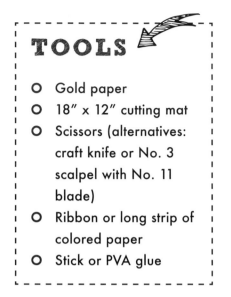

TOOLS

O Gold paper

O 18" x 12" cutting mat

O Scissors (alternatives: craft knife or No. 3 scalpel with No. 11 blade)

O Ribbon or long strip of colored paper

O Stick or PVA glue

When your confidence is shaky, put the medal on to remind yourself you've got what it takes.

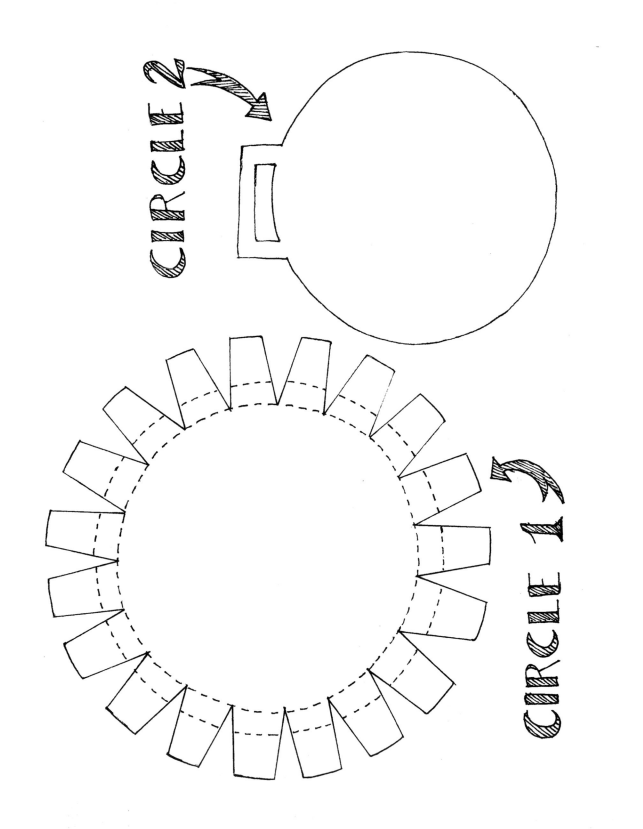

CIRCLE 2

CIRCLE 1

ASK FOR HELP AND HAVE YOUR NEEDS MET

Asking for help can be difficult for those who got the message as children that doing so would result in them being punished, ignored, or rejected. This can lead to a great fear of being refused and an assumption that you will be viewed as weak, needy, or incompetent. There is also added anxiety from the guilt of taking up other people's time and potentially being a burden.

　People with perfectionist tendencies can suffer particularly badly from this problem, as they feel they should be able to cope with everything on their own and can be too ashamed to ask for assistance. But it's so important to remember: it's always okay to ask for help.

+ FIRST STEPS

Even the strongest people need support, and asking for help is *not* a sign of weakness—it shows that you value yourself and are able to take practical steps to have your needs met.

Most people are only too willing to help, but if the person you ask declines, there's no need to take it personally. Just accept it with good grace and view their no as bringing you closer to a yes from someone who will come to your aid.

In the past, you may have developed a victim-type identity in a bid to increase the chances of people saying yes to you, but avoid doing this from now on. It's best to be assertive and straightforward about what it is that you want and why you need help.

If you have more than one thing you need assistance with, it can be useful to make a list of these things, as well as another list consisting of people who could help you with each task— rather than going to one person for help with all of these things.

+ FIRST ART KIT REMEDY

Often people won't offer help to others because they feel they might be intruding or stepping out of line. But people love being altruistic, as it gives them a sense of purpose and well-being, so don't feel ashamed or fearful to ask for help—the majority of people will respond positively.

Do be sure to make your request when the person isn't busy, and don't guilt-trip them with whiny begging or bargaining—just ask straight up: "Could you help me, please?"

If you still feel reluctant, say to yourself "I am as entitled to have my needs met as anyone else, and I need help" before going ahead with the asking.

I've created this old-fashioned gramophone papercraft to remind you that when you speak up, someone will listen. Remember that asking for help is a sign of maturity, and it will also signal to others that they can ask you for help when they need it, too.

METHOD

1. Photocopy or trace the template on pages 68–69 onto printer paper and then cut out all the elements with a craft knife or scalpel. Draw around them onto the colored paper and score all the dotted lines with the back of a craft knife or scalpel blade.

2. Cut out the **Horn** in both red and metallic paper, or any other contrasting colors you prefer. Score along the dotted lines on both **Horn** elements with the back of the scalpel blade and bend at the score marks.

3. Use a couple of pieces of masking tape to hold down the colored paper and the template on top if you're struggling to control the paper while you score it.

4. Bend the red **Horn** into a cone and glue **Flap A** on the outside.

5. Take **Part 1** and curl it around your finger so it bends into a tube, and glue it in place at **Flap A**. Hold in place until dry. Glue the insides of **Tabs B** and stick them onto the outside part of the red **Horn** at the smallest end so that the top of **Part 1** is close up against the **Horn**.

6. Take the gold **Horn** and glue it over the top of the red one, making sure that **Flap A** is on the inside this time. Bend back the scalloped edges so they appear to be face-on when you look into the **Horn**.

7. Bend **Part 2** around your finger and glue at **Flap A**. Hold in place until dry. Glue the outside of **Tabs B** and stick them into the interior of **Part 1** so the **No. 2** tube is at quite a sharp angle. Use a pencil to push the tabs down on the inside.

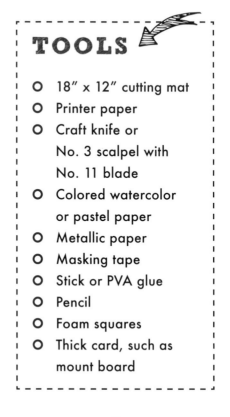

TOOLS

- 18" x 12" cutting mat
- Printer paper
- Craft knife or No. 3 scalpel with No. 11 blade
- Colored watercolor or pastel paper
- Metallic paper
- Masking tape
- Stick or PVA glue
- Pencil
- Foam squares
- Thick card, such as mount board

✚

Now you can fire up the gramophone in your imagination anytime you need to ask for help –someone will always be there to listen.

8. Take **Part 3** and gently pinch **Parts A** while folding **Parts B** over them to make a right angle. Glue **Parts B** in place.

9. Cut the slits marked on **Part 4** and then bend it around your finger, as with **Parts 1** and **2**. Glue at **Flap A**.

10. Cut **Part 5** out of silver card and slide the disc into the slots on **Part 4**.

11. Glue the wide end of **Part 4** into the bottom of **Part 3**, using plenty of glue. Leave to dry.

12. Glue the bottom of **Part 2**—which now forms the lower part of the gramophone horn tubing—into **Part 3**, on top of **Part 4**, which it should be touching.

13. Cut the **Box** out of brown paper and glue **Flaps A** onto the inside of **Parts A**. Do the same with **Parts B** and **C**.

14. Cut the **Handle** out of silver card, glue black paper over the egg-shaped end, and insert into the slot on the **Box**.

15. Stick foam squares on top of one another until they are half a centimeter high. Stick this tower onto the center of the top of the **Box**.

16. Cut the **Record** from black paper and stick onto the middle of the foam squares.

17. Cut the **Spine** from mount board or other thick card and glue to the side of the **Box** opposite the **Handle**. Once that's dry, glue the top of the **Spine** on the same side as before and attach the gramophone tubing up to the top of **Part 2**.

18. Lay **Spine** flat until dry.

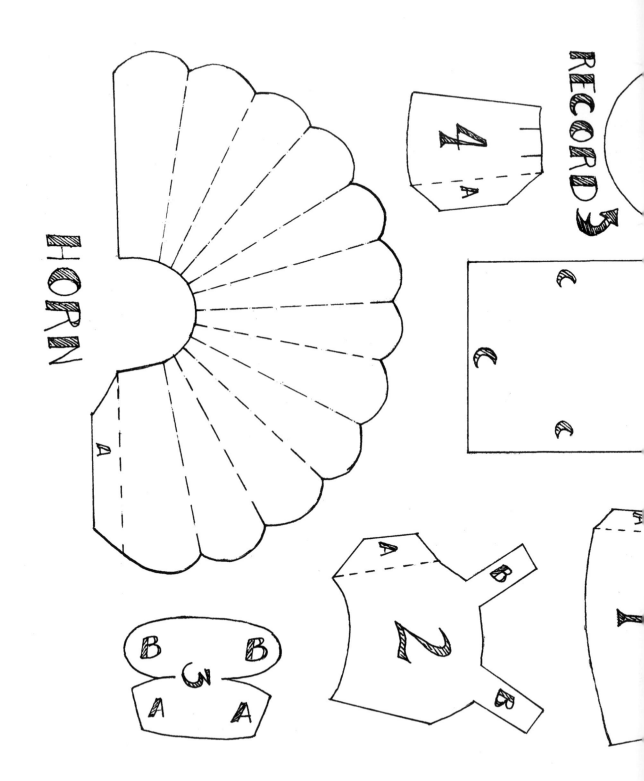

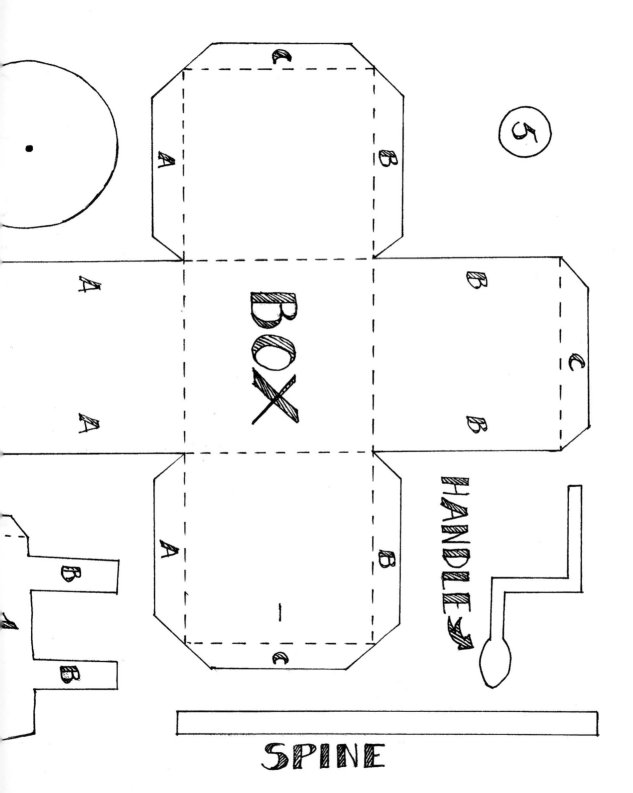

BOX

HANDLE

SPINE

A A A A A A

B B B B B B

C C C

(5)

Thirteen

FIND THE BEAUTY IN IMPERFECTION

Because perfection is impossible to achieve in reality, those who suffer from perfectionism can experience significant problems with their productivity, relationships, and health.

Perfectionism can be caused by overly critical parents or other authority figures who don't tolerate mistakes, or those who praise children only for their achievements rather than their efforts.

People who are perfectionists are terribly self-critical and face high levels of stress from taking on more than they can realistically handle. They also often put off starting projects due to the fear that they might fail, without understanding that there is beauty in imperfection—and we shouldn't spend our lives always trying to avoid it.

+ FIRST STEPS

It's hard to enjoy life when you're always berating yourself for past mistakes or all the things you think you ought to accomplish in the future. One way to overcome perfectionism is to stop measuring yourself in relation to other people.

This comparing mindset only feeds your perfectionist tendencies and almost always leads to negative opinions of yourself. There isn't a level playing field in life—even within families—so it is pointless to do this. Always bear in mind that there is a difference between striving for excellence and demanding perfection. Don't even bother with the latter—it's useless and will more often than not make you unhappy.

+ FIRST ART KIT REMEDY

When you find yourself comparing and thinking things like "That person is so much better than me at X," stop and replace this thought with a more realistic statement, such as "That person is great at X, but I'm great at Y."

Although this may feel false at first, just fake it till you make it. Eventually, the replacement statement will become a new habit. Do it every time you negatively compare yourself to others.

In addition, try to see the situation as others might see it and turn your critical inner voice into a compassionate one you might use with a loved one in the same situation. Then reward yourself for the progress you make by doing something you enjoy.

As a papercraft remedy, I want you to assemble this collage of clocks and flowers. I chose flowers, specifically, because it's the imperfections in the soil that allow them to grow. This craft will also hopefully remind you that we all have a limited amount of time, so it's important to enjoy life as much as you can.

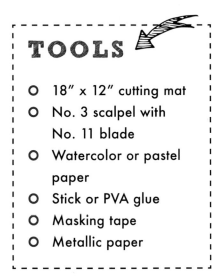

TOOLS

- ⭕ 18" x 12" cutting mat
- ⭕ No. 3 scalpel with No. 11 blade
- ⭕ Watercolor or pastel paper
- ⭕ Stick or PVA glue
- ⭕ Masking tape
- ⭕ Metallic paper

The whole point of this exercise is to show you that there is no "right" way to do things—creativity is fluid. What you might perceive as "mistakes" are just happy accidents, which can lead to new ways of thinking or groundbreaking artworks.

METHOD

1. Trace or photocopy the template on pages 74–75.

2. Cut out each element in the paper color of your choice with a scalpel. These can then be customized in any way you like.

3. Because it's a collage, you can make it look however you want. Disregard some elements, or use others in multiple forms.

4. Assemble it in any way you like—you can have flowers as clock faces or cogs growing out of a stem. Let your imagination run wild!

5. When you're happy with the arrangement of the pieces, glue them in position on a piece of paper.

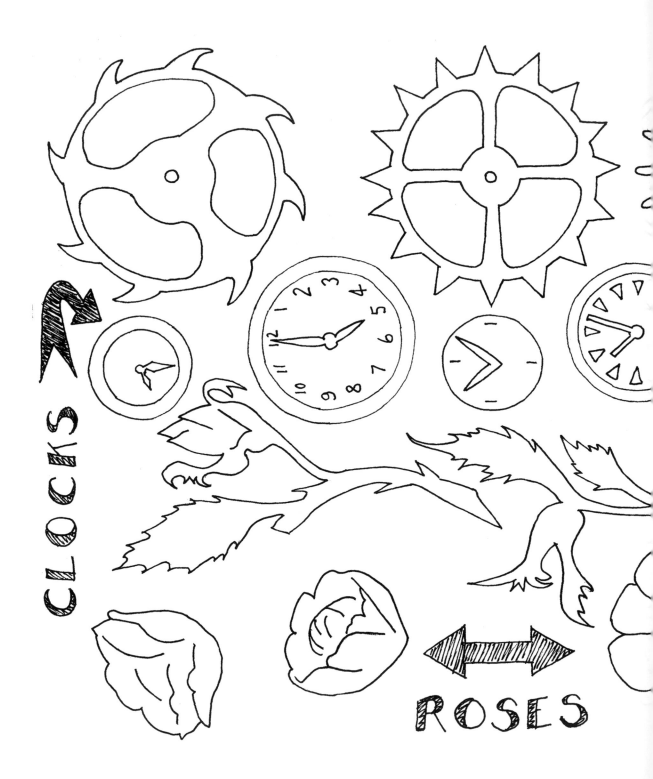

LEAVES

COGS

Fourteen

LISTEN TO AND LEARN FROM CRITICISM

Like perfectionists, people who find it hard to deal with criticism in adult life often had parents who found fault with them as children and didn't praise them for anything they did well.

This type of treatment can lead to anger, defensiveness, or withdrawal in a person, and eventually to a heightened sensitivity to criticism, even if it's constructive.

People who experience this can also start to assume that they don't deserve love or that their skills are of no value, so they avoid any activity at which they might fail. But receiving criticism isn't always a bad thing.

+ FIRST STEPS

Our brains are actually wired to remember criticism, and we're four times more likely to remember negative feedback than praise.[1] So bear in mind that overcoming a fear of criticism is hard, and you deserve to reward yourself when you tackle it successfully.

That said, constructive criticism is helpful and allows you to grow and improve your skills, so try to welcome this, listen carefully to it, and think about the value it contains. Avoid becoming defensive and stay calm during the period of criticism, listening to it objectively. If, on reflection, you feel it wasn't warranted, you can assert yourself later by laying out the reasons why you thought it was unfair.

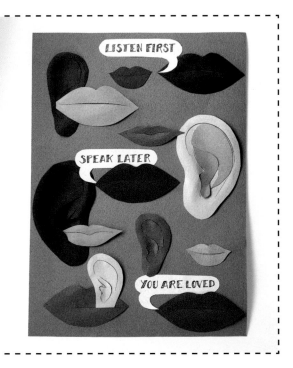

+ FIRST ART KIT REMEDY

After you've received criticism, spend some time weighing whether the criticism was warranted or not. If you ultimately feel it wasn't, then realize it was probably more about the insecurities of the person doing the criticizing than about you, and at this point you should let it go.

Criticism of any kind can cause an adult to have a major psychological crisis. You may end up feeling like you're a terrible person or that the consequences of the criticism are going to be so awful you won't be able to cope. But this is not the case. As an adult, you have agency and the ability to assertively state your case, or just accept that the criticism is useful and can help you improve. No criticism has any bearing on how loved you are.

To help you remember that listening is an important part of coping with criticism, try creating this collage of ears and mouths that remind you to listen first and speak later.

METHOD

1. Trace or photocopy the template on page 79 and cut out the **Ears**, **Lips**, and **Speak Bubble**. Use a craft knife or scalpel to cut fine lines in the middle of the illustrations where these are marked.

2. Holding the ear template over a colored piece of paper, draw around it with a pencil. To make the inner-ear markings, lift **Area 2** with the craft knife or scalpel and draw a line with the pencil along its edge. Do the same with **Area 3**.

3. Now use these marks to cut your ear out of the colored paper.

4. Once it's cut, give the ear shape by using your fingers. **Area 1** can be rolled backward over your forefinger, and **Areas 2** and **3** can be bent backward so they look indented.

5. Treat the **Lips** in the same way, drawing around them, marking the parting between the lips on the colored paper, and then cutting. Finally, bend the paper with your fingers to give a bas-relief effect.

6. Create as many of the items as you like, in whatever colors, and use your skill and judgment to collage and glue them onto backing paper in a way that's pleasing to your eye. There's no right or wrong here—just do whatever works for you.

TOOLS

- O   18" x 12" cutting mat
- O   Craft knife or No. 3 scalpel with No. 11 blade
- O   Watercolor or pastel paper
- O   Masking tape
- O   Stick or PVA glue
- O   Pencil

Once your collage is complete, my hope is that you can feel more confident in your ability to deal with criticism and that you have a craft to remind yourself you have a healthy strategy to practice with criticism anytime you encounter it.

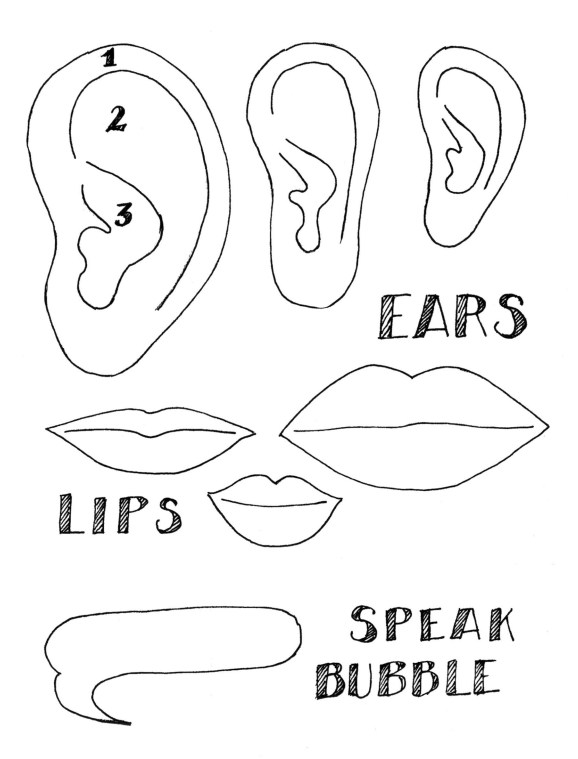

Fifteen

ADVOCATE FOR YOURSELF IN THE FACE OF BULLYING

Being the target of a bully as an adult can be just as distressing as it is for a child. It should never be downplayed, because bullying is a form of mental abuse that can lead to anxiety, fear, and depression.

People learn to become bullies as toddlers, and contrary to popular belief, they tend to be arrogant, with high self-esteem.[1] They attack others to take away feelings of shame they developed in childhood and give themselves an enjoyable jolt of power.

Bullies are not capable of remorse, and they intimidate, control, and shame others by homing in on the insecurities of sensitive people who blame themselves for being bullied. If you have experienced bullying as an adult, I want you to know that you are not alone and there are many ways you can advocate for yourself if you're in this situation.

+ FIRST STEPS

Bullies hate exposure, so the best way to deal with them is to tell others what's been going on. If you're being bullied at work, for example, human resources professionals often recommend you have a trusted confidant witness the bullying, if possible, and log any interactions or communications that highlight it.[2] Your company may also have a policy regarding how to address the issue. If you've followed company policy and have evidence, then you can go to your company's human resources department and make a formal complaint. If human resources does nothing and the bullying persists, you can also speak to a lawyer to explore your options.

Similar actions can be taken if you're being bullied in a friendship group. If you feel strong and safe enough, take your bully aside privately and calmly state that you don't appreciate their behavior—but never tell them how bad they make you feel. Bullies gain pleasure from your powerlessness, and doing this may encourage them to bully you more.

Remember to take care of your mental and physical needs during this time as well, and prioritize surrounding yourself with people who make you happy.

+ FIRST ART KIT REMEDY

With bullies, it's important to remember that their bullying is not about you—it's all about them and their inability to deal with shame and insecurity.

Because bullies choose victims who can't or won't fight back, sometimes the best strategy is to change how you respond to the bully. Former first lady Eleanor Roosevelt once said, "No one can make you feel inferior without your consent," and she was absolutely right!

You can change your body language by pulling your shoulders back, keeping your back straight, and lifting your head up. Be assertive, calm, and professional at all times, as bullies target people they know will get upset by their actions. If the bully says something horrible to you, you can respond: "I'd rather you didn't speak to me like that." If they keep going, you can keep repeating this sentence for as long as it takes. This "broken record" approach is a common one in assertiveness training.[3]

To remind yourself that your needs are as valuable as anyone else's, create and dress this paper doll of Eleanor Roosevelt and keep it close by at work, perhaps as a bookmark or on your desk.

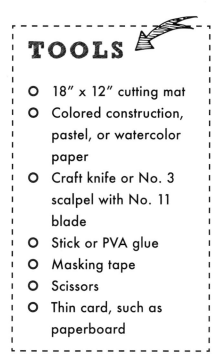

TOOLS

- 18" x 12" cutting mat
- Colored construction, pastel, or watercolor paper
- Craft knife or No. 3 scalpel with No. 11 blade
- Stick or PVA glue
- Masking tape
- Scissors
- Thin card, such as paperboard

✤

Now Eleanor is ready to inspire and help you tell those bullies where to go.

METHOD

1. Photocopy or trace Eleanor's **Body** template on pages 84–85 onto pale pink paper and cut around the outline with the scalpel or scissors. Then cut the line of her chin with a craft knife or scalpel.

2. Photocopy or trace all the other template elements on pages 84–85 onto the paper colors of your choice, and then cut them out. Glue the **Top**, **Skirt**, **Hair**, **Necklace**, and **Shoes** directly onto the **Body**.

3. Cut the **Stand** from a piece of thin card. If you're using paperboard, cover it with colored paper. Score the dotted line with the back of a craft knife or scalpel blade and bend it backward at forty-five degrees.

4. Glue the bottom half of the **Body** to the longest part of the **Stand**.

5. Take the **Coat** and **Hat** and fit them over the **Body**, folding the tabs back along the dotted lines. The bottom tab on the coat can be slotted in behind the **Body** if you avoid gluing the **Skirt** right to the edge.

6. You could also give Eleanor a different selection of clothes using the existing templates as a guide.

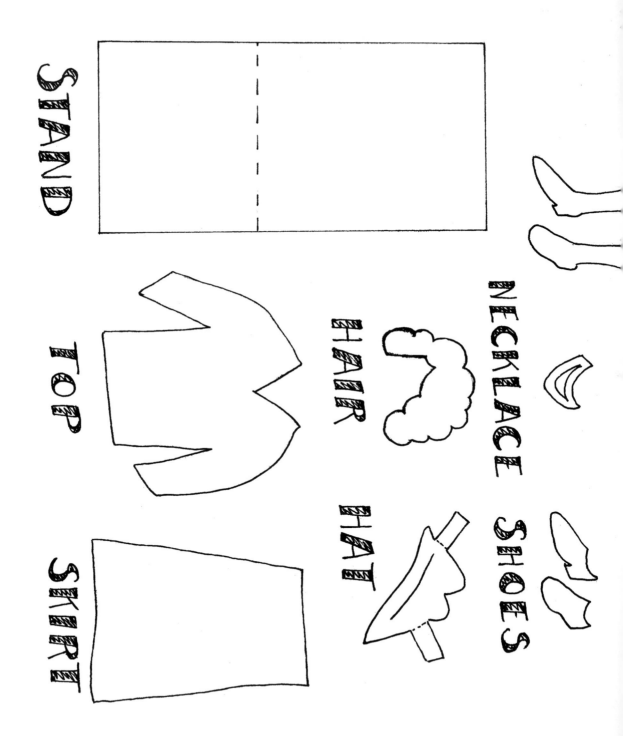

STAND

TOP

SKIRT

NECKLACE

HAIR

HAT

SHOES

BODY

COAT

Sixteen

TURN OFF SOCIAL MEDIA AND PUT DOWN ROOTS

People can become so involved in social networking sites that it causes them psychological distress to be without them, resulting in anxiety, insecurity, restlessness, and anger. But aside from the habit-forming nature of social media itself, the underlying reasons for the overuse of it include loneliness, approval seeking, and low self-esteem.

This constant connectivity actually exacerbates these problems, impacting negatively on relationships, sleep, work, and other responsibilities, as well as preventing us from reaching our goals. If social media is becoming a problem for you, it's worth exploring how to remove yourself from it so you can focus on more beneficial things.

+ FIRST STEPS

Social media is consciously designed to encourage addictive behaviors, as many of us receive a hit of dopamine whenever we get a like or a positive comment. This, in turn, fuels feelings of pleasure and reward, but getting this reward in a more productive, healthy manner is the key to beating social media addiction.

Work out why you use social media in the first place. Perhaps you don't get enough attention in other areas of your life, you're bored, or you feel lonely. Write a list of other ways you could solve these issues in the real world.

It takes three weeks to break a habit, according to Maxwell Maltz's seminal book *Psycho-Cybernetics*, so you could go cold turkey for that length of time or try breaking the social media habit in smaller steps, such as by turning off notifications, temporarily deactivating your accounts, or deleting the apps from your phone.

+ FIRST ART KIT REMEDY

The pull-to-refresh function on apps and red notification dots that show up on app icons when you've received a new like, comment, or message have been shown to increase interaction with these platforms. And it's telling that many of the people who create and control social media rarely use it themselves or let their kids use it.[1]

Replace your checking habit with something else, like reading a book, sketching, handwriting a letter, or some other absorbing pastime that can be dipped into when you'd usually be scrolling through your feed.

If you can't quit social media completely, try to use it only for predetermined amounts of time—thirty minutes during your lunch hour, for example.

As a remedy for this issue, I want you to make a book sculpture of a tree, symbolizing the roots you're going to put down in more productive areas of your life. The time you save on scrolling will also allow other parts of you to grow.

TOOLS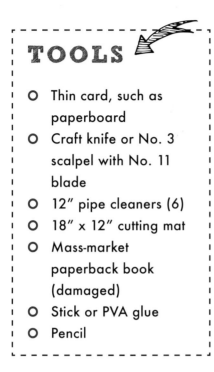

- O Thin card, such as paperboard
- O Craft knife or No. 3 scalpel with No. 11 blade
- O 12" pipe cleaners (6)
- O 18" x 12" cutting mat
- O Mass-market paperback book (damaged)
- O Stick or PVA glue
- O Pencil

✚

With all the time you'll save from not being on social media, you could even make a forest of book trees of varying heights and leaf patterns.

METHOD

1. Photocopy or trace the **Leaf** template on page 91 onto thin card, cut it out with a craft knife or scalpel, and put it aside.

2. Take five of the pipe cleaners and hold them together in a column. Twist them together about ¾ of the way down so there are about 3" left untwisted at the bottom. These will be your roots.

3. Continue to twist the rest of the pipe cleaners upward until the twisted area is approximately 5" long. This will be the trunk of the tree, and the untwisted part above will be branches.

4. Open out the roots and the branches so the tree stands up. Take your final pipe cleaner and cut off sections of varying lengths, then twist these onto the branches to make the tree look fuller.

5. Take your book and tear out about fifteen pages— but don't tear them all from one section, as you will be using the book as a display stand later.

6. Tear some of the pages downward into long strips about 1" wide, and then tear off the ends. Tearing is better than cutting, as you don't want to see sharp edges on your finished tree.

7. Glue the whole length of a strip, and then—starting closest to the trunk—wrap the strip around one of the roots like a bandage until you reach the tip. Do this with each root in turn and double or triple wrap until you reach the desired thickness.

8. For the trunk, the same principle applies, but here you can either use the thin strips as before or use a 5" strip to cover the whole trunk at once, as you can see I did in the photo.

9. It's also easier to apply the strips to the trunk if you temporarily flatten all the branches and roots back into a column until this task is complete.

10. At the ends of the strips that join to the roots and the branches, make multiple small tears so that these open out and provide a more natural-looking join.

11. When you get to the top layer for the trunk, scrunch your paper up and then flatten it out again before applying it to the trunk, to make it look more like bark.

12. Repeat the bandage-wrapping process for the branches.

13. Once this process is complete, you can cover any pieces of pipe cleaner that are still showing by tearing off small strips of paper, gluing well, and applying them as Band-Aids of sorts to the gaps.

14. Open out the roots so the tree is standing straight and arrange the branches into a pleasing configuration.

15. Take the **Leaf** template you created earlier and place it over a stack of three to five loose book pages. Draw around the template with a pencil and then cut out with the craft knife or scalpel through all the pages at once.

16. Carefully detach the design from each page of paper, put a spot of glue in the middle of one set of leaves, and glue to the end of a branch.

17. Repeat this—cutting out multiple leaf sections—until you have the tree as full as you'd like.

18. To finish, open your book flat in the middle and position your tree roots so they're spread out over the pages. One root needs to be stuck in the book crease at the front and another at the back for stability.

Seventeen

FOCUS ON THINGS MONEY CAN'T BUY AND MANAGE SHOPAHOLIC TENDENCIES

Logically, we don't need lots of stuff. But compulsively shopping for things isn't about logic—it's actually about meeting unfulfilled psychological needs.

Buying things can give us an adrenaline rush, allowing us to ignore unpleasant feelings such as depression, anger, loneliness, and low self-esteem, although the purchasing can frequently be followed by guilt, anger, and shame.

People with compulsive shopping or "shopaholic" tendencies often spend money they don't have to cheer themselves up, but the root cause is usually never dealt with—which is why, if you're prone to making impulse purchases, it's important to remember that this behavior will not lead to true happiness.

+ FIRST STEPS

Maybe you get angry or anxious if you are prevented from buying something you want, or you buy yourself things to reward yourself or lift your mood. If you do, that's a problem.

Work out what causes your shopaholic tendencies. Is it pleasure from reward? Or does shopping allow you to avoid negative feelings like disappointment or fear?

Start writing down the trigger every time you get the urge to shop, and decide how you could fulfill these needs in more positive ways.

Ultimately, your goal should be to create robust self-esteem and to refocus your energy on the joy that comes from being around the people you love and from appreciation of the simple things in life.

+ FIRST ART KIT REMEDY

Because happiness doesn't come from buying things, your well-being is likely to decrease if you're a compulsive shopper.

So if you can, cut up your credit cards, try to primarily use cash only, and write down everything you spend for at least a month. You'll be surprised by how many impulse buys you may make, even when you're only carrying cash, and how much you spend on goods that are not essential.

Avoid spending time looking at triggers that encourage you to shop, like window displays, TV or social media ads, online shopping sites, and magazines. And don't go into malls or stores that you know you have a weakness for. When you're poised to make an impulsive purchase, ask yourself: "Would I die without it?" The answer is always no.

I've made these shadow puppets that you can use to represent you and your favorite person. The heart symbolizes your ability to refocus your attention on the things that are truly important instead of shopping, but if you can think of another symbol that is more meaningful to you, do a simple outline of it and use that instead.

Use the figures that most closely represent you and your best friend—you could even use the figures as a base for multiple friends. You can, of course, also customize the characters as much as you like.

TOOLS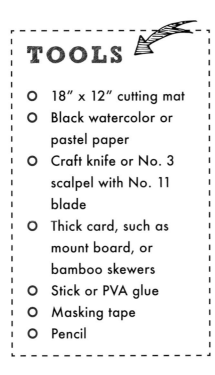

- ○ 18" x 12" cutting mat
- ○ Black watercolor or pastel paper
- ○ Craft knife or No. 3 scalpel with No. 11 blade
- ○ Thick card, such as mount board, or bamboo skewers
- ○ Stick or PVA glue
- ○ Masking tape
- ○ Pencil

METHOD

1. Photocopy or trace the template on pages 96–97 and then cut an oblong around **Fig A** and stick it to the black paper with masking tape.

2. Use a craft knife or scalpel to cut all the lines on the body first before cutting around the outline. Do the same with **Fig B**. The filled-in black areas on both figures should be removed entirely.

3. Cut out the **Heart**, or a silhouette of your own symbol of love and friendship.

4. For the sticks to hold the figures, you can either use bamboo skewers or thick card, such as mount board. For the former, glue a skewer to the leg of each figure and also secure with a couple of small pieces of masking tape.

5. To use mount board, cut strips ⅛" wide and 6" long and glue these to the backs of the figures' legs.

6. Finally, glue the point of the **Heart**—or your preferred symbol—into the hand of one of the figures. By shining a light onto the puppets, you can even create shadows on a wall as the basis for a play.

FIG·A

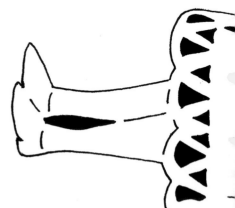

HEART

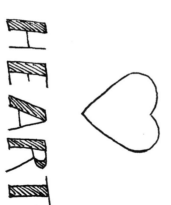

FIG·B

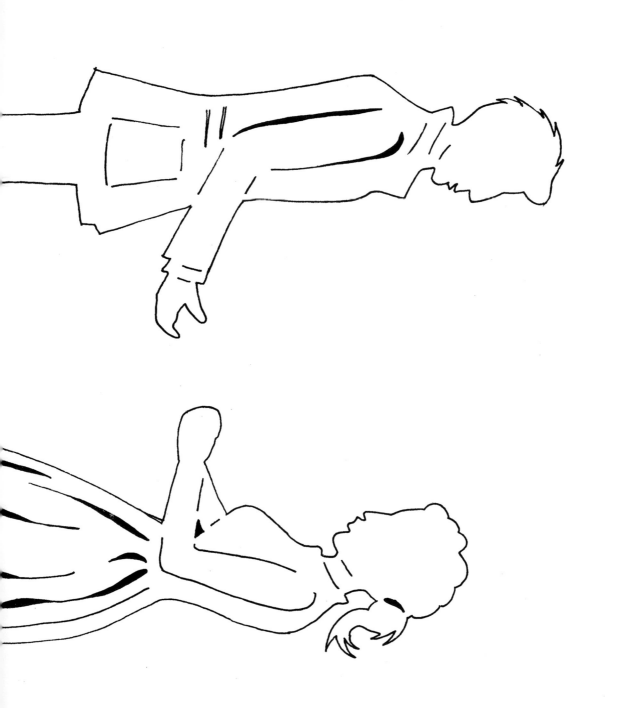

Eighteen

SOAR FREE FROM BLAME AND FORGIVE YOUR PARENTS

One of the most important steps to take on the path to maturity is knowing when to forgive others. Many people who have difficult relationships with their parents tend to struggle with this, but forgiving your parents can release you from the prison of resentment and lead to your own happiness.

Continuing to blame parents for bad things they've done only keeps the pain you experienced fresh and gives them power over your life in your subconscious mind. Unable to live your life until they apologize and give you their unconditional love, you remain a victim, and may never feel worthy of love from anyone.

+ FIRST STEPS

In order to feel compassion for your parents and move on from any resentment you feel toward them, try putting yourself in their shoes and seeing what life was like for them. If they were brought up by unsympathetic, authoritarian parents, then they may have turned out like that themselves.

Know that the way they treated you is a reflection of their own insecurities and upbringing—and try to remember it's not about you; it's about them.

If you want to maintain contact with your parents but still address your issues with them, meet with them to lay out some ground rules about how you—and they—would like to be treated from now on.

At the end of the day, forgiveness is all about respecting people's boundaries, and you are as entitled to be treated respectfully as they are. It may take time for their behavior to change, and you should politely correct them when they slip up, but over time you can forge a new relationship.

+ FIRST ART KIT REMEDY

It's important to remember that most people are doing the best they can given their personal development at the time, and this truism will allow you to have compassion for even the most dysfunctional of parents.

Although your parents may have dealt you a tough hand, you still get to choose whether that affects your whole life or not. You are in charge of the present, and the past does not define you. If you're stuck in the cycle of blame, choose to set yourself free.

Work out how you've benefited from your challenging childhood. Perhaps you have greater empathy, or a keen sense of justice—either way, acknowledge that you wouldn't have these qualities if you hadn't been hurt.

Have zero expectations of your parents—if they didn't meet your needs in childhood, they're unlikely to do so now—and remember that forgiveness is something you do for yourself, not for the person being forgiven.

I've made this collage of papercut butterflies to remind you to let go of blame and soar free.

TOOLS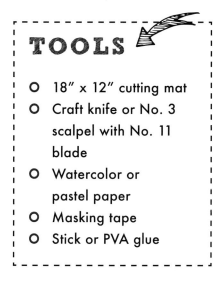

- O 18" x 12" cutting mat
- O Craft knife or No. 3 scalpel with No. 11 blade
- O Watercolor or pastel paper
- O Masking tape
- O Stick or PVA glue

METHOD

1. Photocopy the templates on pages 102–3, and then cut the photocopy into three separate oblongs with a butterfly in the middle of each.

2. Along its edges, tape colored paper that is slightly larger than one oblong in size onto a cutting mat. Make sure there are no air bubbles inside by smoothing it down with your hands.

3. Lay one **Butterfly** template over the paper, taping its outer edges down in the same way.

4. Holding the craft knife or scalpel like a pen, begin cutting around all the black elements from the middle of the **Butterfly** outward.

5. Once you've cut around all the black pieces, carefully peel off the masking tape holding the template down.

6. Then use the tip of the craft knife or scalpel blade to pick out the blanks, cutting a little more where pieces may still be joined to the main body of the artwork.

7. Once all the blanks have been removed, take the masking tape and surplus paper from the mat.

8. Repeat with the other **Butterfly** templates.

9. Once the butterflies are complete, bend their wings up from the body and gently lift the antennae so they look like they're flying.

10. Glue them on the underside of their bodies to a contrasting piece of paper, or you can even use a removable adhesive putty to stick them individually around your home. This way, they can act as a reminder that you can liberate yourself anytime you like; all you need to do is forgive.

Nineteen

SOOTHE YOURSELF
WITHOUT OVEREATING

While occasionally eating comfort foods when
you're sad is normal, overeating as a way to deal
with unpleasant emotions can become an issue for
some people, and depression, anxiety, poor self-
esteem, and perfectionism can all contribute.

When people compulsively overeat, they get
a rush of "happy" chemicals to the brain, which
then leads to psychological addiction. And, like
any addiction, the behavior must be repeated in
order to crush the feelings of guilt and shame that
accompany it.[1]

The shame many emotional eaters and overeaters
feel about their bodies or habits often contributes
to poor self-esteem and makes them feel they will
never be accepted and loved for who they are. So
if you're someone who struggles with this, I want
you to know that there are other, healthier ways
of coping with your feelings, especially in times of
sadness or stress.

+ FIRST STEPS

Emotional eaters are often not aware that their behavior is caused by unwanted feelings, so identifying the root of the problem is key. Think back to incidents—perhaps in childhood—that may have made you unhappy and which you couldn't deal with at the time.

Make an effort then to reduce stress and increase your mental well-being. Our bodies release the hormone cortisol when we're under pressure and this increases our appetite—especially for sugary foods. Sugar, in turn, releases serotonin to make us feel calm and relaxed. Exercise has been shown to suppress appetite and lower stress, so try to incorporate this into your everyday routine by doing things like going for a walk at lunchtime or cycling to and from places if you can rather than traveling via car.

Eating smaller portions—and often—also regulates your blood sugar and ensures you don't get hungry, potentially helping you not to overeat. A couple of portion-control strategies to help you avoid overeating as recommended by registered dietitians include making sure a serving of carbs in any given meal is roughly the same size as your fist and a serving of meat or other protein is roughly the same size as your palm.[2]

+ FIRST ART KIT REMEDY

Start keeping a diary of everything you consume daily, as this can help you notice patterns, such as when you overeat, and situations that may trigger this behavior.

Also try to think of another way to calm your emotions when you feel upset or anxious, such as listening to your favorite song or doing something creative.

As a creative remedy, I've created a double-layer collage for you to make, which aims to help you focus on the real causes of your overeating. As you can see, it's a brain, which has been sectioned off into emotional zones.

On the flaps of each section, write things that may be causing you distress. Underneath these flaps, write words that are the opposite of the unpleasant emotions you may be feeling. For example, if you felt unloved as a child, write "I am loved."

Spend time really working out where this need to soothe yourself with food came from, and concentrate on the new symbols you've created instead.

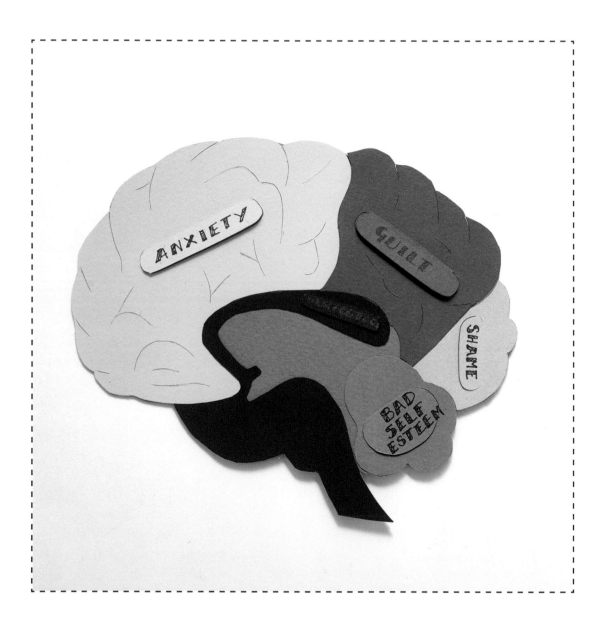

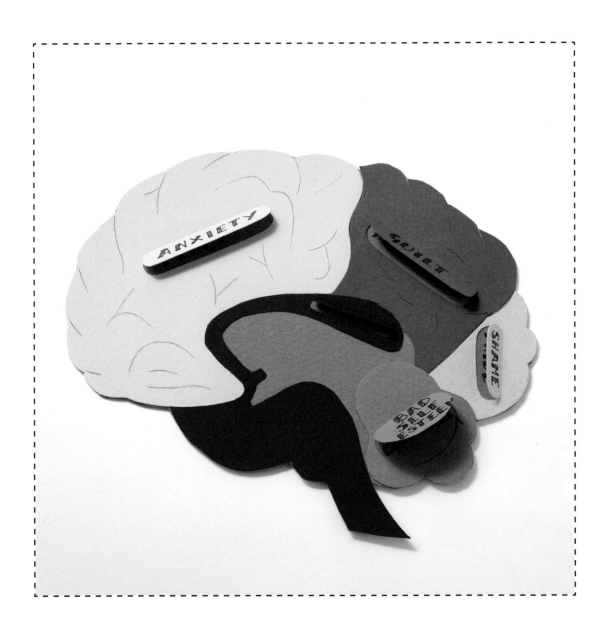

METHOD

1. Photocopy or trace the template on page 109 onto a piece of plain paper and cut around the outer edge of the whole **Brain** with scissors or the scalpel.

2. Using this as a guide, draw around it onto a piece of thin card and cut it out. Choose a piece of colored paper as the base layer of the collage and, again, draw around the **Brain** and cut it out.

3. Glue the paper and card brains together so you have a firm base to work from.

4. Take the template and cut out **Section 1**, colored blue in the photograph. Place it over some colored paper and draw around it with your pencil. Then take a couple of small pieces of masking tape and fix it in position within your pencil line.

5. Cut all the thin lines representing the furrows of the **Brain** with either a craft knife or scalpel and around the line of the flap. Use the back of the blade to score the dotted line, which will act as a hinge.

6. Remove the template and cut around the pencil outline. Gently pull the flap backward to release it. Glue this section around its edges—avoiding the flap—and place in the correct spot on the outline of the brain you made earlier.

7. Repeat this process with the other four sections.

8. When the whole **Brain** is assembled, spend time thinking about which emotional problems might be causing you to overeat and write the five most worrying on the flaps of the brain sections, and then write the opposite, positive words underneath the flaps—these words may be how you feel now, as an adult, or they may represent an emotional goal that you want to work toward.

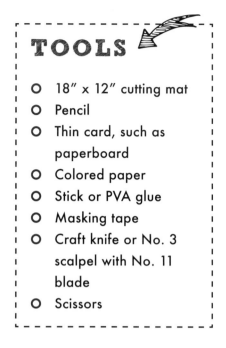

TOOLS

- 18" x 12" cutting mat
- Pencil
- Thin card, such as paperboard
- Colored paper
- Stick or PVA glue
- Masking tape
- Craft knife or No. 3 scalpel with No. 11 blade
- Scissors

✚

Put the Brain on your fridge or a cabinet to remind you that the emotions causing you to overeat can be tackled and needn't hold you back any longer. You are capable of analyzing, accepting, and moving on from them to a happier and healthier future.

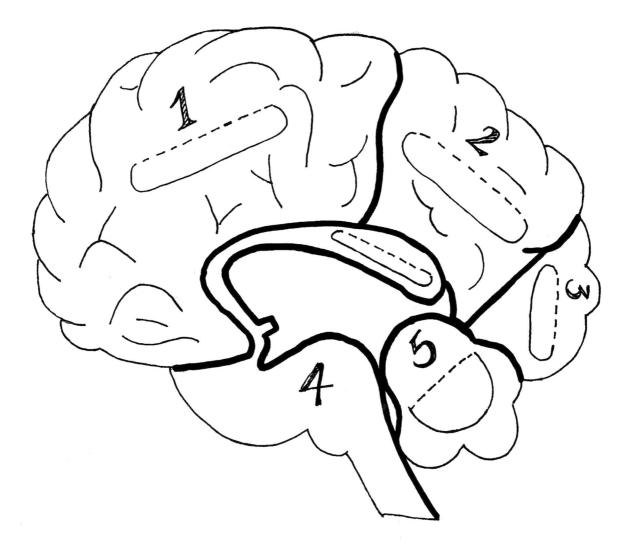

Twenty

LEARN TO SAY NO AND STOP PEOPLE-PLEASING

People-pleasers who can't say no to things they don't want to do often have backgrounds where they felt they weren't good enough and had to earn their parents' affection. Punitive parenting—where children are praised for meeting high standards and punished when they don't—is among the causes of this disorder.

The desire to fit in among our peers is also very strong, and many of us are afraid that saying no will cause conflict or keep others from liking us or hurt their feelings. But it's important to remember that your mental well-being is more important than pleasing others, and no is always an option.

+ FIRST STEPS

The next time you want to say no, ask yourself how bad it will actually be if you say no to what is being asked of you. You may feel guilt, anxiety, or other unpleasant emotions, but there are methods of tackling those.

You can also practice saying no politely but firmly in low-risk situations such as while interacting with a barista in a café or when you're with a friend who can help you act out scenarios that you dread.

In addition, you can try the "sandwich technique," in which you put two positive statements on either side of the no. For example, you say that you understand the other person's need, and you empathize, but you have to decline for whatever reason. Then empathize again by saying you hope things work out for them.

If the person making the request persists, just keep repeating the same thing over and over again in a courteous, patient manner.

+ FIRST ART KIT REMEDY

Remember, when saying no, it's not always necessary for you to have an excuse, apologize, or explain why you don't want to do something. It's enough to just have your opinion and to expect others to respect your needs.

Perhaps the person you're saying no to will be disappointed, but ask yourself if they want someone to lie to them—which is what you'll be doing if you say yes when you want to say no. They could ultimately lose trust in you for not being honest.

People-pleasers can often find themselves in bad friendships or romantic relationships, as they can end up with manipulators who only want to hear yes. This behavior can lead to anxiety, stress, and burnout, because you relinquish all the time for yourself to other people you couldn't tell no.

As a remedy, I've created a cute little book that when you open it pops up to say "Nope!" You can leave it open as a reminder that you are allowed to say that word.

Alternatively, keep it in your bag, and hand it to someone you trust who has a good sense of humor on the occasion you need to firmly but politely say no to them. That way you can raise a smile while also getting your point across.

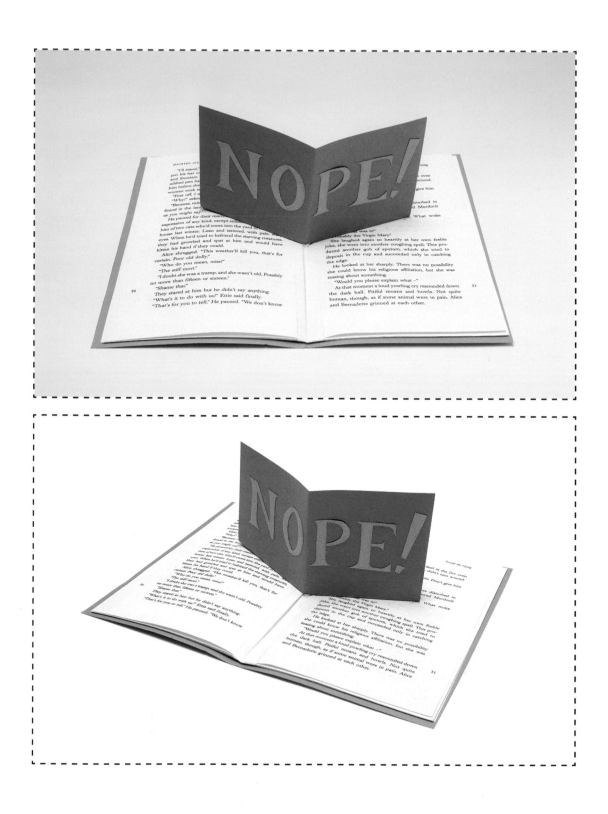

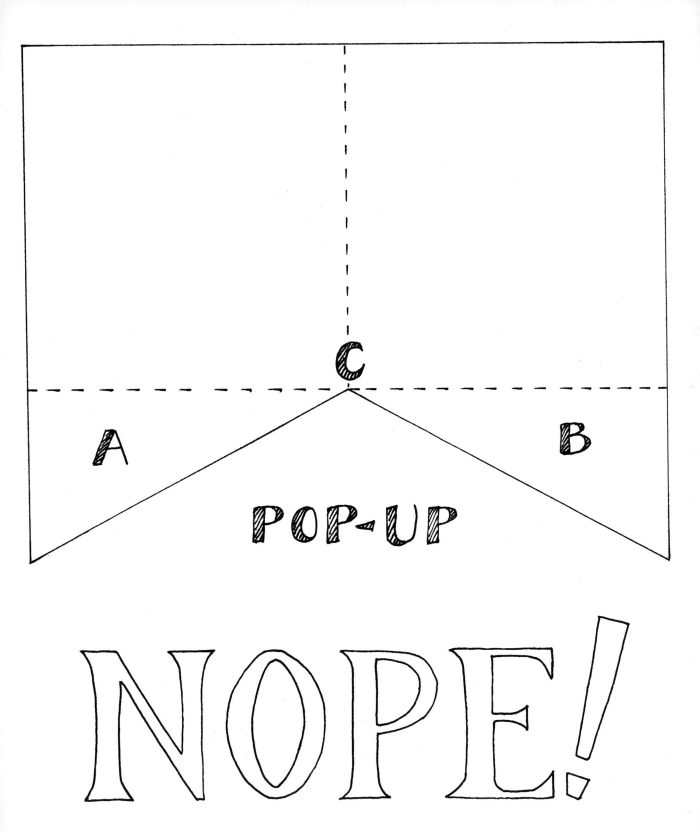

METHOD

1. Trace or photocopy the template on page 113 onto colored paper, cut out, and set aside.

2. Use a craft knife or a scalpel to cut out twenty pages from the paperback, slicing as close to the center line as possible.

3. Arrange the pages in two piles of ten on your mat, with the pages neatly aligned. In between the two piles, take a piece of masking tape that is slightly longer than the length of the pages and curl back the ends so they stick to the mat and the long piece of sticky tape is facing, sticky side up, toward you.

4. Overlap half of your neat pile of pages onto half of the tape strip, and then do the same with the other pile so the pages butt up against each other in the middle.

5. Turn over the ends of the tape to hold down the top and bottom of the pages. Take another piece of tape that's slightly longer than the length of the pages, stick it down the center line, and curl it around at the ends.

6. Close the book to make a crease in the center line.

7. At this point, you can either carefully remove the original book cover and attach it to the newly joined pages or make a new one. To do the latter, open your newly joined book pages onto a piece of colored paper and measure a ¼" space to the sides and ⅛" above the top and beneath the bottom, and then cut around.

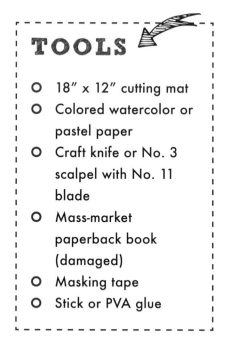

TOOLS

- 18" x 12" cutting mat
- Colored watercolor or pastel paper
- Craft knife or No. 3 scalpel with No. 11 blade
- Mass-market paperback book (damaged)
- Masking tape
- Stick or PVA glue

✚

The book that will teach you how to say "Nope!" to things you don't want to do is now ready for action.

8. Fold the colored paper in half and glue along the center line, which will be your new book's spine. Insert the pages onto this glued line and close the cover around them. Put a weight on top and wait thirty minutes for the glue to dry.

9. Take the **Pop-up** section, fold inward along the dotted lines, and then open out and glue the letters onto the side that folds away from you, making sure that none of the letters touch the center fold.

10. Glue **Flaps A** and **B** on the underside. Open the pages of the new book in the middle and position **Area C** of the **Pop-up**—where all the folds meet— halfway up the book spine, with "Nope!" facing toward you. **Flaps A** and **B** should form a wide V shape. Close the book to check that the **Pop-up** works, and reposition it if necessary before the glue dries.

Twenty-One

FOSTER THE GOOD IN YOU, NOT A VICTIM MENTALITY

People with a victim mentality see life as a series of bad experiences that happen "to" them and which they are powerless to change. This thinking can develop from genuinely traumatic experiences, perhaps in childhood, and it allows the sufferer to gain sympathy and attention while avoiding feelings of suppressed anger.

Victim mentality also ensures sufferers never have to take responsibility for their lives or take action to improve their lot, which in turn can impede their ability to live a happy and fulfilling life.

+ FIRST STEPS

Start by prioritizing your needs and saying no to things you don't want to do. Remember that you are as entitled as anyone to have your opinions respected.

Then write down all the things you're grateful for, be kind to yourself, and stop the practice of blaming others. By remaining a victim, you are intensifying your pain, not soothing it.

Aim to help other people, either with random acts of kindness, volunteering, or assisting those in your own friendship group. This will change the narrative that you're a helpless victim.

Though it can feel very hard to do, try to forgive those who have wronged you, as holding on to anger can become exhausting and only harms yourself.

+ FIRST ART KIT REMEDY

A person with good mental health knows that when misfortune or tragedy strikes, it often has nothing to do with whether they deserve it or not: it's random. They also realize that many events—good or bad—can happen because of choices they make. If you are someone who suffers from a victim mentality, then this is the stage you need to get to.

If you remain a victim, you'll get to hold on to a little bit of power, but you'll ultimately be stressed out and unhappy, without the capability to reach your full potential.

As a remedy, I want you to create a papercraft inspired by an insightful Native American story, which you may have heard of, about the two wolves within us.

As the story goes, a grandfather tells his grandson there is a constant battle between two wolves going on inside us all. One of the wolves inside us is bad and expresses anger, envy, jealousy, sorrow, regret, greed, arrogance, self-pity, guilt, resentment, inferiority, lies, false pride, superiority, and ego.

The other wolf, however, is good and expresses joy, peace, forgiveness, love, hope, serenity, humility, kindness, benevolence, empathy, generosity, truth, and compassion.

When the grandson asks his grandfather which wolf wins the battle, the grandfather replies: "The one that you feed."

With this wisdom in mind, by making this lupine papercut I want you to remind yourself to feed only the good wolf inside you.

METHOD

1. Trace or photocopy the templates on pages 121–23, and then draw around them onto the appropriate colors of paper and cut out. To copy my colors, use pale brown for **Head** and **Chin**; pale gray for **Beard**, **Eyes 1**, and **Inner Ears**; black for **Eyes 2**, **Mouth**, and **Nose**; yellow for **Pupils**; and dark brown for the **Sides**.

2. On the **Head**, use a craft knife or scalpel to cut the continuous lines in the middle of the template, and use the back of the craft knife or scalpel blade to score the dotted lines. Remove the template and gently lift up **Area 1**, curving it around your finger.

3. Bend **Area 3** down at a 30-degree angle. Lift **Area 2** upward and curve the sides downward. Lift **Area 4** upward.

4. Bend the **Ears** toward you and push one of your thumbs into the middle of each ear to make a dent.

5. Take the **Beard** and score along the dotted lines before bending it backward to make cheeks.

6. Glue the **Inner Ears** into position, as seen on the photo.

7. Put glue on the **Beard**'s lower portion only, so as not to affect the bend of the cheeks. **Area 4** on the **Beard** goes right up to the line of **Area 4** on the **Head**.

8. Glue the **Mouth** on top of **Area 4** on the **Head**, and glue the **Nose** onto **Area 3**.

9. Glue the **Chin** onto **Area 4** of the **Beard**.

TOOLS

- 18" x 12" cutting mat
- Watercolor or pastel paper
- Craft knife or No. 3 scalpel with No. 11 blade
- Stick or PVA glue
- Wite-Out (optional)
- Foam squares
- Black felt pen

✚

Your Good Wolf is now ready to be fed.

10. Take **L Eye 2** and glue onto **L Eye 1**, as seen on the photo. Do the same with **R Eye 2** and **R Eye 1**. Glue an **Iris** into the center of each eye and draw a pupil onto it with your pen. A dot of Wite-Out can be used to create the reflection.

11. Put foam squares on the rear of these completed eyes and fix them onto the **Head** in the position shown.

12. Finally, glue the **Side Furs** into position behind the **Head**—using the **L** and **R** indicators for the left and right sides.

L·INNER EAR   R·INNER EAR

L·EYE 1

R·EYE 1

IRIS

L·EYE 2   R·EYE 2

MOUTH

NOSE

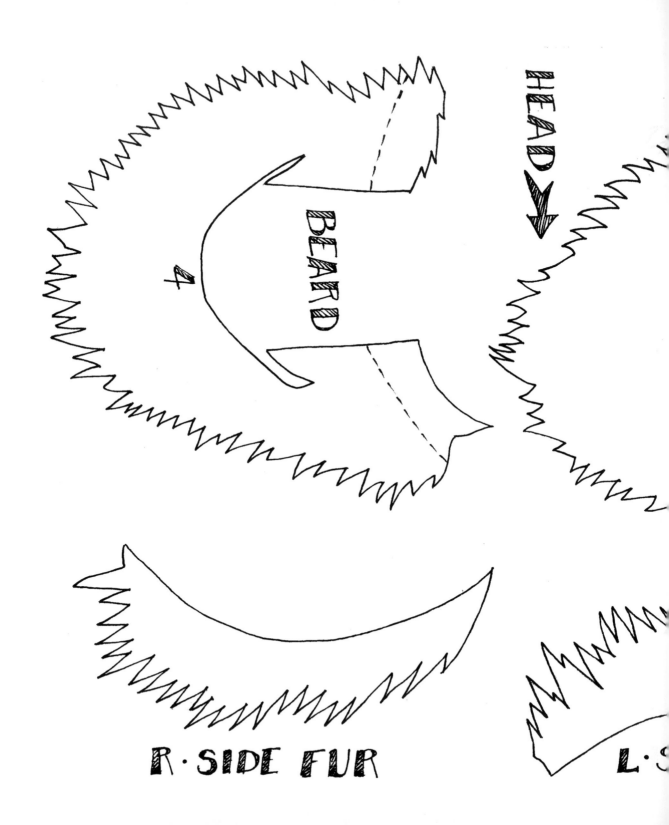

HEAD ➤

BEARD

4

R·SIDE FUR

L·S

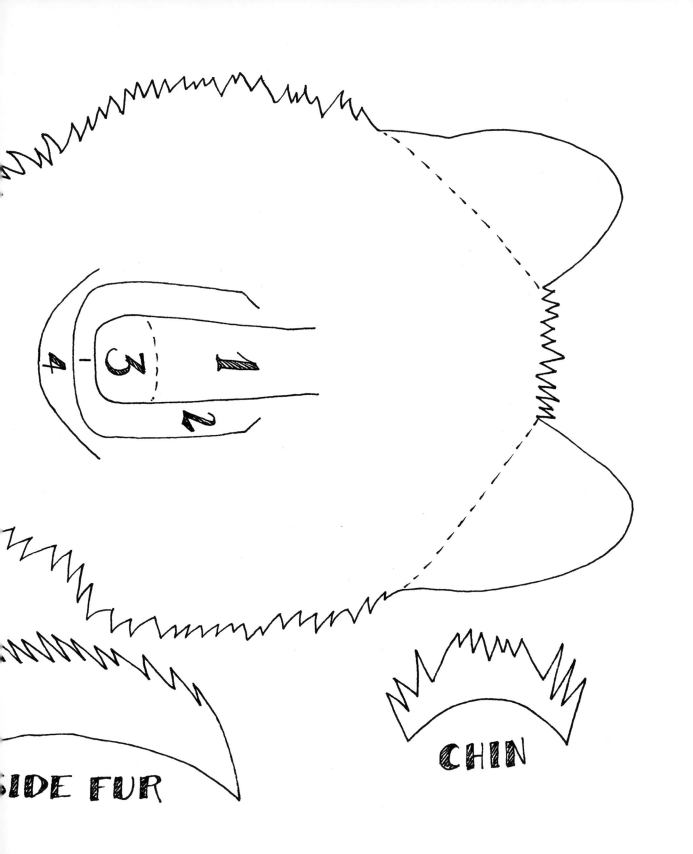

4 3 1 2

SIDE FUR

CHIN

 Twenty-Two

THINK OF THE BEST-CASE SCENARIO AND CURB YOUR CATASTROPHIZING

Catastrophizing is the habit of exaggerating the negative parts of any situation or imagining that if one thing goes wrong, everything will. It releases adrenaline and cortisol—which has been linked to heart disease, obesity, osteoporosis, depression, and high blood pressure—so this behavior can potentially damage your health as well as your happiness.[1]

If your upbringing made you feel unsafe, for example, then you will continue to be hypervigilant and anxious as an adult, which in turn leads to low self-esteem and an inability to reach your goals. But you don't need to live this way, and I want you to know that whatever outcome you may be stressing about is usually not as likely or as bad as you think.

+ FIRST STEPS

The most important way to break this habit is to start separating fact from your own fiction. Try to notice when you're engaging in catastrophic thinking and interrogate whether your thoughts are actually based on reality. Usually, there are multiple different outcomes possible to any given scenario.

When you find yourself leaping to the worst-case scenario, with the panic rising in your chest, start listing all the possible alternative outcomes—especially the positive or neutral ones.

Merely having "a feeling" about a situation is not proof of facts. You can't, for example, get inside someone else's head and know their thoughts, their motivations, and their hurdles on any given day, so it's pointless trying to predict what they'll do.

Physical exercise or doing a craft or pastime that requires concentration have both been shown to be effective in reducing anxiety, as they can bring people back to the present and give them relief from thoughts about the past or future.

+ FIRST ART KIT REMEDY

Catastrophizing can be a self-fulfilling prophecy—raised cortisol means poor judgment, which in turn can lead to negative outcomes. So when you feel that surge of adrenaline, stop what you're doing and remind yourself that this reaction isn't about the current situation; it's really about what happened to you in the past.

Soothe yourself at the earliest opportunity by doing something you enjoy, and know that—even in the unlikely event that your catastrophized worst-case scenario were to come to pass—you will survive.

With this in mind, I want you to hand-make a journal in which you can write down all the best-case scenarios when you are in a catastrophizing state of mind. This will not only train your mind to consider alternative outcomes but also give you an object of which you can be proud. The mere act of making it will help you to escape catastrophic thinking as well.

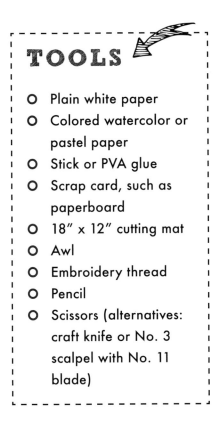

TOOLS

- Plain white paper
- Colored watercolor or pastel paper
- Stick or PVA glue
- Scrap card, such as paperboard
- 18" x 12" cutting mat
- Awl
- Embroidery thread
- Pencil
- Scissors (alternatives: craft knife or No. 3 scalpel with No. 11 blade)

✚

Carry the journal with you during the day so you can tackle catastrophic thinking when it occurs. You can also use it for sketching, to take your mind away from any anxious thoughts.

METHOD

1. Take ten sheets of white paper—I've used 10" x 7" paper, but you can adapt these measurements to make any size of journal you like—and fold each sheet in half with a sharp line. Then open them out and compile them into one big wad.

2. Take the colored paper you want for your cover and measure it ¼" bigger all around than your opened-out pile of white paper.

3. Cut a contrasting strip of colored paper that is 1" x 10". Place on top of the cover and fold ends under. Glue in place.

4. Open your stack of white pages and mark three evenly spaced dots, about 1½" apart, down the center fold with your pencil.

5. Place a long strip of scrap card on your mat—if you're using paperboard, place three strips on top of each other to make it thicker. Place the cover's spine over the scrap paperboard or card, and then place the white pages on top of that so they're exactly in the middle.

6. Take your awl and press down hard through the three dots you made so it punctures through all the pages and the cover.

7. Thread a large needle with embroidery thread and push through the center hole from the pages side, leaving 3" of thread hanging out.

8. Return the needle through the bottom hole, and then through the center hole, top hole, center hole, and bottom hole. Cut off thread, save for 3". Tie ends of the thread together at center hole in a double knot.

9. Cut off loose ends.

Twenty-Three

TREASURE WHAT'S REALLY IMPORTANT INSTEAD OF HOARDING

The compulsion to continually accumulate things and the inability to give them up, also known as hoarding, is an issue for many people. There are varying degrees of hoarding—sparked by multiple risk factors—but the one thing hoarding behaviors have in common is that they relieve the hoarder's anxiety by insulating them from the outside world.

Humans become attached to objects at a very young age, and because of this we tend to place more value on a thing simply because it is ours. As we mature, we can also begin to link our self-worth to objects to make ourselves feel more important, and this can lead to great distress if we lose them or have to give them up, so it's important to understand how letting go of excess stuff can actually help you if you have hoarding tendencies.

+ FIRST STEPS

Consider working out what emotional need you're trying to satisfy through your attachment to things, and then find a different way to fulfill that need.

Holding on to stuff is our way of filling an emotional void. But once we've created a comfortable living space, the continued collecting of things can actually create stress due to the fear of the loss of those things.

Once you've identified why you're doing this, you can slowly start every week to clear out one small area of your home, a place where you store things, starting with clearing out the things you feel the least attachment to and that serve no functional purpose.

Try thinning out collections of the same thing to just one or two of the best items and recycle, donate, or sell the rest.

+ FIRST ART KIT REMEDY

Studies have shown that people get greater satisfaction from experiences than from things.[1] So I encourage you to consider selling your excess stuff and spending the money you earn from the sale on experiences instead.

A good general rule is that if you haven't used or looked at an item for over a year, let it go. Having fewer things is a form of liberation that frees you from the anxiety and guilt of ownership, which includes responsibility for the insuring, the looking after, the cleaning, the storing, and the sorting.

What are the top ten things you prize more than anything else? Once you've decided, you can move on to clearing out the clutter that does not have the emotional significance of those objects.

I've created a treasure chest that symbolizes a small space for your most cherished possessions. As you construct it, think about your ten most important possessions and why you've chosen those over all your other things. This will allow you to see that not everything you own holds the same emotional value, and that you can let a lot of the rest go.

TOOLS

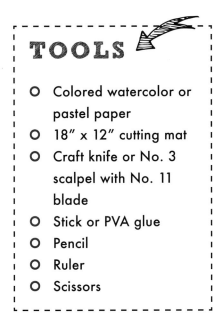

- Colored watercolor or pastel paper
- 18" x 12" cutting mat
- Craft knife or No. 3 scalpel with No. 11 blade
- Stick or PVA glue
- Pencil
- Ruler
- Scissors

✚

Once the Chest is complete, you can fill it with paper representations of your ten favorite things to keep you on track for letting go of any surplus possessions.

METHOD

1. Photocopy or trace the **Chest** template on pages 132–33 onto colored paper. I used paper with different colors on each side.

2. Use the back of a craft knife or scalpel blade against a ruler to score all the dotted lines on the **Chest**, and then cut wherever there is a continuous line.

3. Glue **Flaps A** to the underside of **Parts A1**, holding in place until the glue sets. Glue **Flaps B** to the underside of **Parts B1**. This forms the base of the **Chest**.

4. Glue **Flaps C** to the underside of **Parts C1**, following the curve of **C1** to form the lid. Fold the lid back so the hinge is engaged. Fold **Part D** under, toward the inside of the lid.

5. Cut out the **Strap** from a contrasting colored paper and fold it along the dotted lines before bending the middle over your finger to give it a curve. Glue the heart-shaped ends onto the body of the **Chest**, making sure that the catch on the lid will fit underneath it.

6. Use the **Brace** template to cut out four strips of contrasting paper. Glue these at intervals across the lid.

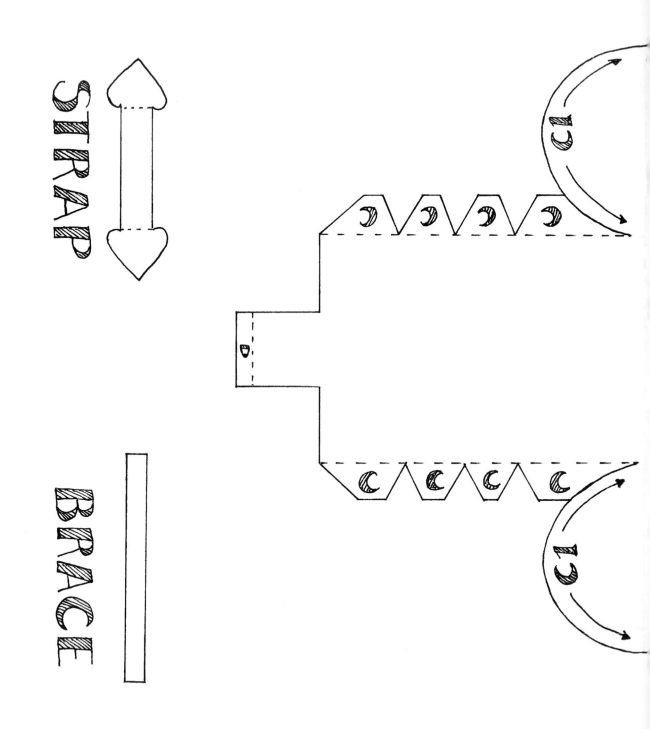

STRAP

BRACE

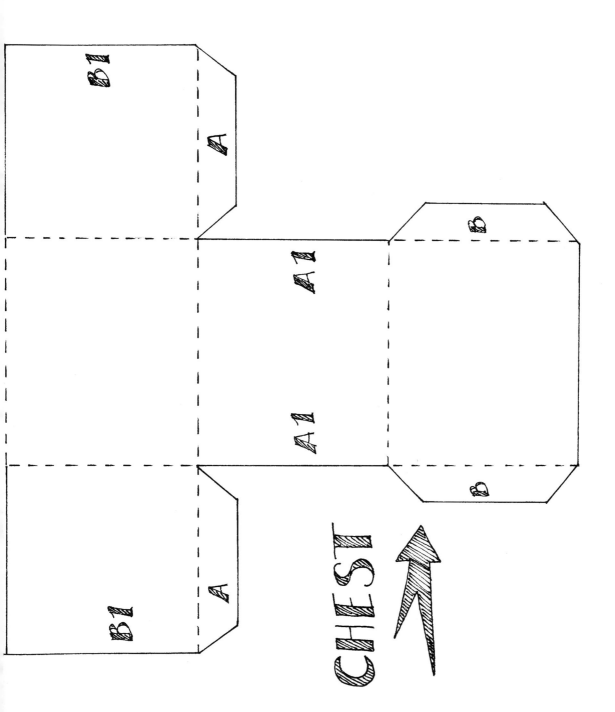

CHEST

Twenty-Four

FIND PEACE WHEN YOU'RE ANGRY

The state of feeling angry all the time has very little purpose other than to soothe the psychological turmoil caused by childhood pain, which is triggered by scenarios in the adult world. It allows us to avoid guilt and fear by making us feel powerful and in control instead.

Anger even releases a hormone that acts as a pain reliever and provides an adrenaline rush that can make us feel invincible, when in reality that is the opposite of how we really feel. However, there are strategies you can implement in order to find peace in times of anger.

+ FIRST STEPS

Given that anger is fundamentally about insecurity, it's a good idea to explore the true cause of your angry outbursts.

Did you have a childhood where an adult humiliated you or made you scared? Get to the bottom of this problem and you're halfway there. Your rage isn't really about what's happening now, it's about what happened then.

Start to notice when you feel your anger rising so you can nip it in the bud before it goes out of control. Remove yourself from the anger-causing situation and go for a walk.

Try to turn the anger into words instead of action by writing down exactly why you are furious, how the other person has made you feel, and what childhood memory is the true trigger for the anger.

+ FIRST ART KIT REMEDY

There is a well-worn saying that holding on to anger is like drinking poison and expecting the other person to die. It's certainly true; anger will ruin you long before it ruins the object of your fury. So if it serves no useful purpose, deal with it and discard it.

When you feel your face getting hot and the red mist descending, remove yourself from the situation and start breathing slowly and deeply from your diaphragm. Put a hand on your stomach; you should see your hand rising and falling when you're doing this correctly.

Close your eyes and focus on your hand rising and falling on top of your diaphragm. When you feel calmer, imagine yourself in a beautiful sunny garden where multicolored flowers burst around you, filling the air with wonderful scent.

Visualize yourself walking along the manicured lawns, listening to the sound of birds singing and reaching out to touch the velvety petals of roses.

I've created a paper nature scene to remind you to head for the garden in your mind to escape the prison of anger.

METHOD

1. Trace or photocopy the template on page 137.

2. Tape watercolor or pastel paper that is larger than your tracing to your mat along its edges. Make sure there are no air bubbles inside by smoothing it down with your hands.

3. Lay the **Bird** template over the paper, taping its outer edges down in the same way.

4. Holding the craft knife or scalpel like a pen, begin cutting around all the black elements from the middle of the picture outward.

5. Once you have cut around all the black pieces, carefully peel off the masking tape holding the template down and remove.

6. Then use the tip of the craft knife or scalpel blade to pick out the blanks, cutting a little more where pieces may still be joined to the main body of the artwork.

7. Once all the blanks have been removed, take the masking tape and surplus paper from the mat.

8. Pick up the bird scene and gently fold or pinch the paper to give a 3D effect to the elements you want to stand out, such as the leaves and flower heads. Attach to a contrasting piece of paper using spray mount adhesive or foam squares.

TOOLS

- O Watercolor or pastel paper
- O Masking tape
- O 18" x 12" cutting mat
- O Craft knife or No. 3 scalpel with No. 11 blade
- O Spray mount adhesive or foam squares
- O Printer paper

+

Now imagine the bird singing, the bees buzzing, and the fresh air in your lungs.

Twenty-Five

UNLOCK ALL THE POSSIBILITIES WITHIN YOURSELF AND DISCOVER SELF-ACCEPTANCE

Self-acceptance is often confused with self-esteem, but they are not the same. The latter is about feeling like you are a good, worthy person, but the former is about accepting yourself, including all your faults, without judgment.

You will have reached self-acceptance when you don't try to diminish or ignore any defects that you think you have in your personality or looks, and I want to assure you that reaching that place is entirely possible.

+ FIRST STEPS

It goes without saying that hating who you are, or even elements of who you are, does not result in a life brimful of joy.

Sometimes our inability to accept ourselves stems from regret that we didn't become who we thought when we were younger that we would be when we grew up. But you must grieve these lost childhood ambitions and focus your energy on the present.

I encourage you to perform small, random acts of kindness regularly, as this will help you understand that you are an important and valuable member of society.

+ FIRST ART KIT REMEDY

Cultivating good psychological health is a marathon, not a sprint, and it's wise to incorporate ways to improve or maintain your psychological health into your everyday life.

This maintenance program should become as habitual as brushing your teeth or taking a shower so that, eventually, you don't even have to think about how you will work it into your everyday routine. Self-acceptance should absolutely be one of the things that's included in this daily maintenance.

One way to achieve this is by keeping a journal of all the things you've accomplished and all your triumphs over adversity, because this can act as a defense against your tendency to focus on your less flattering traits.

Once you have unconditional self-acceptance, you can then start working on other areas of your mental health that may need improvement, safe in the knowledge that your faults do not define you.

To help remind you of the importance of self-acceptance, this papercut shows a lock and key turning to release all the possibilities within you, just as you are.

METHOD

1. Trace or photocopy the template on page 141.

2. Tape metallic paper that is slightly larger than your tracing to your mat along its edges. Make sure there are no air bubbles inside by smoothing it down with your hands.

3. Lay the **Lock** template over the paper, taping its outer edges down in the same way.

4. Using either a craft knife or scalpel, begin cutting around all the black elements from the middle of the picture outward.

5. Once you have cut around all the black pieces, carefully peel off the masking tape holding the template down and remove.

6. Then use the tip of the craft knife or scalpel to pick out the blanks, cutting a little more where pieces may still be joined to the main body of the artwork.

7. Once all the blanks have been removed, take the masking tape and surplus paper from the mat.

8. Select pieces of colored paper, hold one of them under each striped area in the metallic paper, and use a pencil to draw an outline of each. Cut this out about 3 mm from the pencil line so it overlaps the metallic paper.

9. Erase the pencil lines, glue the edge it is to be fitted to, and attach it to the rear of the metallic paper.

10. Do this with each stripe of color.

11. Glue around the rear outer edge of the metallic paper and fix to a darker backing color.

TOOLS

- Masking tape
- Metallic paper
- 18" x 12" cutting mat
- Craft knife or No. 3 scalpel with No. 11 blade
- Watercolor or pastel paper
- Pencil
- Eraser

+

Now you're ready to unlock the good and bad and move forward with self-acceptance.

ACKNOWLEDGMENTS

I WOULD LIKE TO THANK the many people who made this book possible, not least my editor, Lauren Hummel, and all those at Tiller Press who contributed their considerable skills, in particular art director Patrick Sullivan and designer Jennifer Chung, who so brilliantly brought my original concept for the book to life. Kudos also to PR and marketing supremos Laura Flavin, Lauren Ollerhead, and Michael Anderson. I would also like to thank my friends Claire Rodgers and Shawna Mullen for their enduring support, encouragement, and help over the years. But I reserve the biggest thanks for my agent, Joy Tutela, who is always ready to give it to me straight, and whose exotic life stories even manage to surpass mine.

NOTES

SIX: RECOVER FROM REJECTION AND RISE LIKE THE PHOENIX
1. Ethan Kross et al., "Social Rejection Shares Somatosensory Representations with Physical Pain," *Proceedings of the National Academy of Sciences of the United States of America* 108, no. 15 (April 12, 2011): 6270–75, https://doi.org/10.1073/pnas.1102693108.
2. Emma Young, "Rejection Massively Reduces IQ," *New Scientist*, March 15, 2002, https://www.newscientist.com/article/dn2051-rejection-massively-reduces-iq/.

NINE: FORGIVE YOURSELF AND RELEASE SHAME
1. "Habits Shape Your Life!" World Counts, https://www.theworldcounts.com/happiness/psychology-of-habits.

TEN: BRIGHTEN UP YOUR SPACE AND SHAKE OFF SAD
1. "Overview: Seasonal Affective Disorder (SAD)," NHS, July 30, 2018, https://www.nhs.uk/conditions/seasonal-affective-disorder-sad/.

ELEVEN: REMIND YOURSELF YOU ARE A CHAMPION AND BUILD UP YOUR CONFIDENCE
1. Kim Elsesser, "Power Posing Is Back: Amy Cuddy Successfully Refutes Criticism," *Forbes*, April 3, 2018, https://www.forbes.com/sites/kimelsesser/2018/04/03/power-posing-is-back-amy-cuddy-successfully-refutes-criticism/#68eb71083b8e.

FOURTEEN: LISTEN TO AND LEARN FROM CRITICISM
1. Kendra Cherry, "What Is the Negativity Bias?" Verywell Mind, April 29, 2020, www.verywellmind.com/negative-bias-4589618.

FIFTEEN: ADVOCATE FOR YOURSELF IN THE FACE OF BULLYING
1. "Bullies Have Higher Self-Esteem, Social Success Study Finds," CBC News, July 30, 2015, https://www.cbc.ca/news/canada/british-columbia/bullies-have-higher-self-esteem-social-success-study-finds-1.3173387.
2. Crystal Raypole, "How to Identify and Manage Workplace Bullying," Healthline, April 29, 2019, https://www.healthline.com/health/workplace-bullying.
3. "Assertiveness," Wikipedia, https://en.wikipedia.org/wiki/Assertiveness.

SIXTEEN: TURN OFF SOCIAL MEDIA AND PUT DOWN ROOTS
1. Alex Hern, "'Never Get High on Your Own Supply': Why Social Media Bosses Don't Use Social Media," *Guardian*, January 23, 2018, https://www.theguardian.com/media/2018/jan/23/never-get-high-on-your-own-supply-why-social-media-bosses-dont-use-social-media.

NINETEEN: SOOTHE YOURSELF WITHOUT OVEREATING
1. "Food Addiction," WebMD, https://www.webmd.com/mental-health/eating-disorders/binge-eating-disorder/mental-health-food-addiction.
2. Jennie Agg, "Your Hands Hold the Secret to Avoid Overeating," *New York Post*, December 2, 2015, https://nypost.com/2015/12/02/your-hands-hold-the-secret-to-avoid-overeating/.

TWENTY-TWO: THINK OF THE BEST-CASE SCENARIO AND CURB YOUR CATASTROPHIZING
1. Kara E. Hannibal and Mark D. Bishop, "Chronic Stress, Cortisol Dysfunction, and Pain: A Psychoneuroendocrine Rationale for Stress Management in Pain Rehabilitation," *Physical Therapy* 94, no. 12 (December 2014): 1816–25, https://www.ncbi.nlm.nih.gov/pmc/articles/PMC4263906/.

TWENTY-THREE: TREASURE WHAT'S REALLY IMPORTANT INSTEAD OF HOARDING
1. San Francisco State University, "Buying Experiences, Not Possessions, Leads to Greater Happiness," *ScienceDaily*, February 17, 2009, https://www.sciencedaily.com/releases/2009/02/090207150518.htm.